ep *Focus on the Marathon*

Focus on the Marathon

John Humphreys and Ron Holman

EP Publishing Limited

This book is dedicated to our families, for putting up with our obsession with long-distance running

Text copyright © John Humphreys, Ron Holman 1983
Chapter 5 copyright © Ian Adams 1979, 1983

ISBN 0 7158 0847 8 (casebound)
ISBN 0 7158 0848 6 (paperback)

British Library Cataloguing in Publication Data
Humphreys, John
    Focus on the marathon.
    1. Marathon running
    I. Title   II. Holman, Ron
    796.4'26   GV1065

    ISBN 0-7158-0847-8
    ISBN 0-7158-0848-6 Pbk

First edition 1983

Published by EP Publishing Limited, Bradford Road, East Ardsley, Wakefield, West Yorkshire, WF3 2JN, England.

Printed and bound in Italy by Legatoria Editoriale Giovanni Olivotto, Vicenza.

Design: Douglas Martin Associates

Typeset in Great Britain by PFB Art & Type Limited, Leeds, England.

Illustrations: Stephen Beaumont

Contents

Foreword

Ron Hill B.Sc.(Tech), Ph.D., M.B.E.

When as a boy I ran my first ever race for my club, Clayton-le-Moors Harriers, a 2-mile cross-country, little did I know that I was setting out on a career which would span three decades and beyond, and take me on to that most gruelling of events, the marathon. Little did I know in September 1956, when I began to keep a training log, that this log would eventually document over 100,000 miles of training and racing; nor could I know on 21 December 1964 that from that day to this I would never miss a day's running.

In my first marathon, the Liverpool City Marathon of 1961, there were 51 entrants listed on the programme, and obviously fewer than that number started and finished the race. Now we are in the age of the mass marathon, and I am very happy to be a part of that.

My beginnings were in the 'dark ages' of the marathon when little was known of the event except that it was a long, long way and that at about 18 miles your legs started to hurt a lot! We had never heard of 'the wall'. And yet in the famous Polytechnic Marathon of 1964, from Windsor to Chiswick, Basil Heatley (Coventry Godiva Athletic Club), who later that year took the silver medal in the Tokyo Olympic Marathon, ran 2:13.55 to win, whilst I finished second in 2:14.12. Both these are respectable times even by today's standards. Basil held a World's Best time for a short four months until Abebe Bikila of Ethiopia won the Olympic Marathon in 2:12.11.

To improve on such times as these, one had to be a pioneer, and my contribution to the marathon event has been in the design of clothing, notably the mesh vest and 'freedom shorts', and in the application of the 'glycogen loading' diet to this long-distance race.

This book, *Focus on the Marathon*, presents pretty well everything there is to know about the event in one book, and cuts out the most wasteful part of pioneering — the mistakes. I made many of these along the way, probably the most costly being in 1972 when I was still 'refining' the carbohydrate-loading diet, cutting down my intake of carbohydrates to practically zero for four days and doing myself a lot of harm.

The majority of my 100,000-plus miles of training were solely aimed at becoming a better racer, whether it was on the track, cross-country, on the roads or in the marathon. At the beginning, little was known of the health benefits of running, both mental and physical, but these are now fully documented and are well described in this book.

Like life, training and racing have their ups and downs. A recent 23-mile training run in high winds and pouring freezing rain had me doubting the wisdom of such excursions, but running in the sun and the green of summer in just a pair of shorts more than makes up for that!

Now that scientific evidence has proved what I have always felt, that running keeps a person in excellent physical condition, I will continue for the rest of my life. This book will be a valuable companion if — as I hope you will — you decide to do likewise.

Ron Hill

Introduction *Ron Holman*

At 26 miles and 385 yards (approximately 42km), the marathon is the longest run in the Olympic Games.

There was no such event in the ancient Olympics: the marathon was added to the modern games by their founder, Baron Pierre de Coubertin, in 1896, one of the Olympic delegates having offered a trophy to commemorate the historic run of the Greek soldier Pheidippides from Marathon to Athens in 490BC, bearing news of a resounding Greek victory over the Persians. Pheidippides collapsed and died after his feat, thereby setting a tradition of dramatic conclusions to the marathon.

The distance over which the race is run has varied between 40 and almost 43km (Pheidippides' run was about 35km long); it was only at the 1908 Olympic Games, in London, that it was standardised. The course was planned to cover 26 miles, from the grounds of Windsor Castle to the White City Stadium, but an extra distance of 385 yards was added on so that the finish could take place in front of the Royal Box, where Edward VII was to be present.

Olympic marathons

From the first the marathon, which traditionally takes place at the end of the Olympic Games, has provided controversy, tragedy and scenes as dramatic as any in the cinema. By the end of those first Olympics, in Athens, no Greek had won a medal, and patriotic businessmen were offering not only cash prizes but also such odd inducements as free shaves for life to any native of the host country who could salvage Greek pride by winning the marathon. There were only seventeen starters, none of whom had run the distance before, and they not only had to contend with a rather too hospitable crowd lining the route but were accompanied much of the way by a detachment of Greek cavalry, whose prime function seemed to be to stir up dust. The victor was a Greek shepherd, Spiridon Louis, whose legs were no doubt inspired by the thought of all those prizes.

The marathon has always had, too, its share of 'characters'. One such was Felix Carjaval, a postman from Cuba, who begged in Havana for his boat fare to the USA, and then jogged and hitch-hiked across the continent to St Louis, where the 1904 Olympics were being held. Clad in his street clothes, he lined up with the others at the start; a helpful member of the Irish team clipped his trousers to just above his knees using a pair of garden shears. The temperature was 90 degrees in the shade and the humidity was high, but these conditions did not bother Carjaval unduly: he ran easily and stopped several times to chat to spectators, pick apples, and accept other fruit offered to him from the roadside. The fruit proved his undoing for, as he was nearing the finish, he suffered severe stomach cramps and slowed, eventually coming in fourth. The winner, Tom Hicks — who although born in Birmingham, England, was competing for the USA — was reportedly given injections of strychnine and several eggs and glasses of brandy during the race. He required the services of four doctors afterwards. Only about half of the starters finished the course.

The 1908 games, held in London, saw what was probably the most dramatic marathon finish ever. Again it was run on a hot, humid day, and again approximately half of the competitors were unable to finish. As the leader entered the stadium to run the final lap, he began to stagger from side to side and even turned to run in the wrong direction. Officials redirected him, but shortly afterwards he fell to the track, obviously suffering from heat exhaustion. He was helped to his feet and sent on his way. This scene was to be repeated twice more before the small, spent figure of the Italian confectioner, Dorando Pietri, finally crossed the line. Pietri was disqualified for receiving assistance, and the gold medal went once more to the USA — to John Hayes, who attributed his lack of heat exhaustion to having spent much of his early life working in the high temperatures of the family bakery. Pietri spent the next two days in hospital, but on his release was given a special cup by Queen Alexandra in recognition of his courage.

Four years later, in 1912 in Stockholm, the problem of heat raised itself yet again and, as well as the by now usual drop-out rate, a Portuguese competitor, Kamed Lazaro, collapsed and the next day died in hospital. The fatality forced the Olympic authorities to introduce the requirement at the next games, in Antwerp, that all marathon runners had to undergo a physical examination before competing. This was the first such medical requirement in Olympic history.

Also from around this time, the nature of marathon running began to change. The days were past when athletes entered the race on whim: runners trained specifically for what had come to be regarded as the supreme athletic test. Although World War I interrupted the sequence of the Olympics, in 1920 they were re-established: in this year, at Antwerp, Hannes Kolehmainen of Finland ran a time of 2 hours, 32 minutes and 35.8 seconds to win the marathon on a course almost 800m over 42km. Two Olympiads later Mohammed el Ouafi, a French-Algerian, provided an omen for the future by becoming the first African to win the event, and further evidence of things to come was given by the performances of the Japanese athletes who finished in fourth and sixth positions. By 1932 and the Los Angeles games, Juan Carlos Zabala of Argentina was able to clip almost another minute off the fastest time for the distance, thereby approaching even more closely the magic two-and-a-half-hour barrier.

The barrier was finally breached in 1936 at the Berlin Games by Kitei Son of Japan. Zabala led in the early stages but was in bad trouble by the time he reached the 28km mark. He was caught here by Son and by Ernest Harper of the UK, but staggered on for a further 4km before retiring. From this point on, the little Japanese relentlessly pushed ahead, finally entering the stadium over two minutes in front of Harper to take the gold medal.

The full drama and appeal of marathon running were captured for posterity in the magnificent sequence during Leni Riefenstahl's film of these games. Enormous attention was paid to Son's unusual footwear, which featured a separate compartment for each big toe, but virtually no regard was given to his training methods, which, as we now know, were paving the way ahead for future runners.

Having provided the winner (and the man in third place, Sharyu Nan) in Berlin, the Japanese were to continue to be a major influence on marathon running. Although their first performance below the 2 hour 20 minute mark was not to be recorded until 1961, by the following year they had 7 such times, and by 1965 they had 27. Japan pioneered the winter marathon, with events such as the Fukuoka in December and the Beppu in February, and often provided the winners in both of these events as well as in many of those held elsewhere, such as the Boston marathon, the Kosice event in Czechoslovakia, and the UK's Polytechnic marathon.

After World War II had provided a further interruption to Olympic proceedings, London saw in 1948 what was almost a re-enactment of the Dorando Pietri incident. Less than 300m covered the first three runners to enter the stadium. First in was the Belgian, former paratrooper Etienne Gailly, but he was wobbling from side to side of the track: he was passed first by Cabrera the Argentinian and then by the Welshman Tom Richards, representing the UK. Gailly at least crossed the line without assistance, thus gaining the bronze medal.

The 1948 games saw also the first appearance, albeit in the track events, of two future 'legends' of the marathon, Emil Zatopek and Jim Peters.

Zatopek, a Czech Army Officer, was to astonish the athletics world four years later in Helsinki by winning the 5,000m, 10,000m and marathon, all in Olympic record times. His win in the marathon was, amazingly, his first run in the event, although he covered prodigious distances in his daily training. The Czech paced himself brilliantly, lying fourth behind the leader, the UK's Jim Peters, at 5km, and third, still behind Peters, at both the 10 and 15km marks. He moved in front at 20km (just under halfway) with the Swedish runner,

Emil Zatopek in 1979 as a guest of the New York marathon

Jansson; 10km later Zatopek had a lead of about 120m, and this he gradually increased until he had built it up to the best part of a kilometre by the time he entered the northern outskirts of Helsinki. He ran into the stadium some two and a half minutes clear of Gorno of Argentina, the second man, clipping over six minutes off the Olympic record in the process. The stadium audience rose as one to salute one of the greatest distance runners of all time.

Jim Peters paid for setting such a blistering pace in the early part of this race: he retired shortly after the 30km mark suffering badly from cramp. His time of glory was yet to come.

Stars of the marathon

An Essex-based optician, Jim Peters had been inspired in his early days by Jack Holden, a successful track and cross-country runner who turned to the marathon late in his career. In the years preceding World War II, Holden had been an eminent cross-country runner, between 1932 and 1936 always being in the first three in the international championships, winning three times during that period and again in 1939. He competed in the 1948 Olympic marathon, but retired with stomach cramp and badly blistered feet. (While Holden was running in the London Olympic marathon, Jim Peters competed in the 10,000m, finishing ninth.) This served only to inspire him to greater efforts: two years later, in 1950, he had a magnificent season, with five marathon wins, including the gold medals at both the Empire Games in New Zealand and the European Championships in Brussels.

Peters, following his disappointment in Helsinki, gradually increased his training, and in 1953 he set new world's-best times for the marathon distance with runs inside 2 hours and 19 minutes. By 1954, his training had increased to the point where he was running nearly 200km in ten sessions per week, much of which he carried out at racing pace. Indeed, in the ten months leading up to the 1954 AAA championship race — where he set yet another world's-best time, 2 hours, 17 minutes and 39.4 seconds — Peters ran almost 7,200km.

After these exploits, it was hardly surprising that he started as favourite in the 1954 Empire Games marathon in Vancouver. Despite intense heat and oppressive humidity, he set off at a startling pace. The announcement was made to the awaiting stadium that the leading runner was over a mile ahead of the next competitor, but appeared to be in trouble. When, several minutes later, Peters entered the arena, the spectators were totally unprepared for the dramatic scene that unfolded before them. Staggering and wobbling, falling to the track and then picking himself up again, he made his desperate way towards the finish. At times the courageous Englishman was actually crawling on all fours during his tortured attempt to cover the distance. Finally, watched by a shocked crowd, he crossed the line — but unfortunately it was the wrong one (it was that used for some of the track events). Acting under instructions from the team management, the physiotherapist rushed forward and assisted the exhausted Peters from the track. He was rushed to hospital in a waiting ambulance.

Later he was presented by the Duke of Edinburgh with a specially struck gold medal inscribed 'to J. Peters as a token of admiration for a most gallant marathon runner'. But once more he had met failure, and he was never to run seriously again. The dehydration and subsequent hospitalisation profoundly affected him — psychologically more than anything — and he retired from active competition. However, he remained a source of inspiration to marathon runners ever afterwards.

In 1960 another upset, although not a tragic one, was to occur in a major marathon. In Rome the Ethiopian runner, Abebe Bikila, a member of Haile Selassie's Imperial Guard, took the Olympic title in a new world's-best time of 2 hours, 15 minutes and 16.2 seconds; incredibly, he covered the entire distance without shoes. It transpired later that this had been his third run over the distance in three months — he had clocked 2:39.50 and 2:21.23 in July and August respectively in the altitude of his native country. Training under the guidance of an expatriate Finnish coach, Oni Nikkanen, Bikila used the intensive continuous running methods of Jim Peters with a blend of more sophisticated interval training, and he carried out his entire programme over mountainous tracks at high altitude.

Bikila was followed home by three Africans in the next seven places, thus disproving the previously held theory that the black races were unsuited to endurance events.

Four years later, Bikila successfully defended his title in Tokyo, this time wearing shoes and winning by over four minutes from a top-class field of distance runners to set yet another world's-best time, 2 hours, 12 minutes and 11.2 seconds. This performance would have stood the test of time by itself but, amazingly, occurred only five or six weeks after the Ethiopian had undergone an appendix operation. In full view of the stadium — not to mention the television audience — Bikila, after finishing, went through a series of callisthenic exercises on the grass inside the track.

Sadly, this great African had to withdraw from the 1968 Olympic race at ten miles (16km) suffering the after-effects of a leg injury; his fellow-countryman, Mamo Wolde, retained first place for Ethiopia. And even sadder events were to come in Abebe Bikila's life. In 1969, he was severely injured in a car accident and suffered spinal injuries which led to paralysis and confinement to a wheelchair. He died some four years later as a result of a brain haemorrhage, still paralysed from the waist down despite intensive treatment.

The late '60s were to see an even more vigorous trainer than either Peters or Bikila. Derek Clayton, a Lancashire-born Australian, rather taller and heavier — at 1.88m and 73kg — than the average top-class marathoner, burst upon the scene. Covering vast distances in his weekly training runs, often to a total of over 300km, Clayton veered between superb performances and horrendous injury. Turning to the longer distance after a reasonably successful track career, he suffered a ruptured Achilles tendon less than two years after his debut in the event. It is all the more astonishing, therefore, that in Japan less than twelve months after this catastrophe he turned in the magnificent time of 2 hours, 9 minutes and 36.4 seconds for the distance, clipping two and a half minutes off the world's best of the time.

The following year he underwent yet more surgery, this time for the removal of a damaged cartilage, yet he still managed to finish seventh in the oxygen-rarefied atmosphere of the Mexico Olympics. In 1969, the surgeon's scalpel interfered with his preparations once more before he ran at Antwerp an amazing 2:8.33.6. (A debate still continues today about the accuracy of the measurement of the course for this run.) Despite very good track speed, and an impressive ability to function at almost full effort for the complete distance, Clayton's approach to training, in terms of both its extent and its intensity, was to prove his undoing. He did not finish in either the 1970 or the 1974 Commonwealth Games, and he was placed no higher than thirteenth in the Munich Olympics after yet more injury problems.

Throughout this era the UK, although not carrying off the major prize of an Olympic title, had produced many excellent marathon runners. Basil Heatley had wrenched the silver medal from the Japanese Tsuburaya in Tokyo, passing him some 100m from the tape, and Brian Kilby had a record five successive wins in the AAA championship event between 1960 and 1964. During this time Kilby took the Commonwealth title in Perth, Australia, in 1962 and also the European gold medal in Belgrade the same year, as well as taking fourth place in the 1964 Olympic marathon.

Ron Hill, a textile research chemist, was another member of the UK marathon team in the 1964 Olympics, finishing in a disappointing nineteenth place. His turn was to come, however; with a solid history of cross-country wins and shorter-distance road-running records behind him, including world's-best performances over 10 and 20 miles (16 and 32km), he entered his greatest period in 1969-70. Following a communication from a UK track international, the biologist Martin Hyman, Hill explored the possibilities of a carbohydrate-boosting dietary regime based on research carried out in Scandinavia and widely reported in scientific journals. In hot, humid weather he took the European title

Ron Hill today, now a world-class veteran marathon runner

in Athens in 1969, moving into the lead less than a kilometre from the finish and maintaining his tempo until he crossed the line, a very fresh-looking victor. He continued his run of successes the next year, winning the Boston marathon in record time (2:10.30) and capping a magnificent season with a tremendous run of 2:09.28, the fastest time ever by a European, to win the Commonwealth Games gold medal in Edinburgh.

As well as the diet mentioned earlier, Hill popularised the cut-away shorts and string vests which are so common today among marathon runners everywhere. He was an innovator, with a scientific mind which would investigate anything that might help him in his quest for faster times. This went to such limits that he appeared at the Munich Olympics in 1972 dressed in silver reflective running gear — described by the eventual winner, Frank Shorter, as Hill's 'space costume'.

Frank Shorter, 1972 Olympic marathon victor, was also an accomplished track runner (no. 807)

Shorter (who, coincidentally, had been born in Munich) took the 1972 title by use of the tactic of running a very fast 5km stretch between 10 and 15km, which took him from eleventh place into a five seconds' lead. He increased this lead by keeping up his relentless pace over the section of the race from 15 to 20km, by which time he held a commanding advantage of 31 seconds. Throttling back slightly, but having done the damage, Shorter won by over two minutes, averaging just over five minutes and two seconds per mile for the entire distance.

Until Frank Shorter's win, US marathon runners were a breed not to be taken too seriously — indeed, the great Emil Zatopek had gone on record as saying that they did not train hard enough, the most serious exercise they took being to walk to their garages! Shorter, however, had admirable credentials for top-class marathoning: he had been an excellent cross-country runner during his college days at Yale, and developed his track speed while a law student at the University of Florida. Rather taller than average, at 1.80m, he weighed only about 59kg. Before his marathon win he had come fifth in the 10,000m in a new US record of 27 minutes and 51.4 seconds (his compatriots, Moore and Bacheler, did their bit to enhance the reputation of US distance runners by finishing fourth and ninth respectively). Undoubtedly Shorter's rather unexpected success led to the running boom in the USA; Americans were no longer the poor relations in distance-running terms, and from coast to coast people began jogging — in parks, along sidewalks, and up and down beaches.

The man who succeeded Shorter was a 27-year-old student, Bill Rodgers. Rodgers had finished well down the field in the 1974 Boston marathon, in a time just inside two hours and twenty minutes, and was fifth the same year in the New York event in outside two and a half hours. By 1975, however, he had

Bill Rodgers receives his 1979 New York award from Zatopek

somehow transformed himself into another runner altogether. After coming third in the World Cross-Country Championships in March, he ran almost ten minutes faster than his previous best to win the Boston marathon, his third attempt, not only winning by nearly two minutes but breaking both Shorter's us record and Ron Hill's course record at the same time.

In the five years between 1975 and 1979, Bill Rodgers won the New York marathon four times and the Boston event three times, as well as being placed third and first in the prestigious Fukuoka race in Japan. Three of his New York wins during this period were by over two minutes, all against world-class opposition including Frank Shorter, Canada's Jerome Drayton, and Ian Thompson of the UK. Seven times he clocked under two hours and twelve minutes for the classic distance and, despite a poor showing in the 1976 Olympics, where he was suffering from a foot injury, he demonstrated a yearly consistency at a level that may never be equalled.

Waldemar Cierpinski

Waldemar Cierpinski, a 26-year-old physical training instructor from East Germany, thwarted Frank Shorter's attempt to retain his Olympic title in Montreal in 1976. In Moscow, four years later, Cierpinski ran a beautifully judged race in trying conditions of high humidity to become only the second man to win the Olympic title in two successive games (Abebe Bikila had been the other). The East German had carried on the by now established tradition of good-class, if not international, track-distance runners moving into the marathon field. He had been an international steeplechaser before moving up to the 10,000m in 1973; he had a best time of 8:32.8 for the steeplechase and of 28:28.2 for the longer distance.

Little was heard of him between his two Olympic wins, the first of which saw him clipping over two minutes from Bikila's Olympic record. Apart from a fourth placing in the 1978 European Championships, Cierpinski kept a very low profile, and this led many to underestimate his chances in Moscow, where he entered the stadium looking remarkably fresh and ran a last 200m in just over 33 seconds to repeat his Olympic triumph. He has been extremely reticent about his training methods and claims to be ignorant of the famous glycogen-boosting diet used by many successful marathoners. However, personal observation in Moscow indicated that his training was conventional by today's standards for world-class runners.

Women in the marathon

At the 1967 Boston marathon, Kathy Switzer gatecrashed the race and finished the course despite the attempts of the organiser physically to remove her. This began a series of attempts by women to break into the marathon. The women's liberation movement allied itself to the cause on a world-wide basis, making its voice particularly heard in the USA.

The first official women's marathon race was held in Waldniel, West Germany, in September, 1974. Won on her home territory by Liane Winter, it demonstrated the increasing strength of Europe's female marathon runners. By 1978 the women's world's-best time for the distance was down to 2:34.18, but then Norway's Grete Waitz, moving up from a successful track career, slashed 2 minutes and 18 seconds off this in the New York event. The following year she was to take an even bigger slice off, with an amazing 2:27.33, which placed her sixty-ninth in a field of 10,602 finishers.

The UK has contributed Joyce Smith to the ranks of pioneering female marathoners. Smith turned to the longer distance after having for many years represented her country at cross-country and track; she ran in the 1,500m in the Munich Olympics, and before that had competed as a serious athlete since she had been 17 years old, beginning as a sprinter and long jumper and then later moving on to middle-distance running, winning the English cross-country title in 1959. Between working part-time as a wages clerk and giving birth to and bringing up two girls, she attacked the marathon with a vengeance. In May, 1982, she improved on her 1981 time by 14 seconds to win the women's section

Joyce Smith

of the Gillette London marathon in 2 hours, 29 minutes and 43 seconds — at the age of 44.

Grete Waitz's time in the 1979 New York marathon would have won every Olympic marathon up to 1948, gained her a bronze medal in the 1956 event held in Melbourne, Australia, and won the New York marathon in both 1970 and 1972. It represents an average pace of under 5 minutes and 40 seconds per mile.

Women had first competed in the Olympic Games in golf and tennis, having been barred from them for many centuries — even as spectators! Subsequently other sports were opened to them, such as swimming, gymnastics and track and field athletics. In 1984, the first women's Olympic marathon race will take place in the Los Angeles games, and the objections of very many years — which would appear to have been based largely on aesthetic grounds and supposed physiological limitations — will have been overcome. Women have arrived on the marathon scene and are clearly here to stay.

Marathons for the people

Although Frank Shorter had stimulated a running boom in the USA, nothing similar happened in the UK until the late '70s, despite the successes of Ian Thompson who, within four months of winning his first marathon, won the Commonwealth crown with a time of 2:09.12, winning the European title later in the same year.

The New York marathon had begun in Central Park in 1970 with a field of 126 runners. By 1976, when it moved onto the streets of the city, the numbers had swelled to 2,000. In the 1981 event this figure had grown to an enormous 14,496 competitors, over 13,000 of whom finished the distance. The first 49 finishers broke 2 hours and 20 minutes, and 187 runners had times inside two and a half hours.

The 1981 New York marathon: runners cross Verrazano bridge

The inaugural London marathon in 1981, brain-child of former Olympic steeplechasers Chris Brasher and John Disley, captured the hearts of the British, and of Londoners in particular. By 1982 the second London event, sponsored by Gillette, had, even by the admission of Fred Lebow, the organiser of the New York marathon, overtaken the US event as a 'people's marathon', with over 16,000 entries, 93 per cent of them finishing the course. By comparison with the previous New York race, only 30 runners ran faster than 2 hours and 20 minutes, but nearly 200 broke two and a half hours.

Hugh Jones, here seen winning the British students' 10,000 metres at Meadowbank, Edinburgh, in 1979, went on to win the 1982 London marathon in the very fast time of 2 hours 9 minutes 24 seconds

Two runners who have benefitted from the authors' advice, heading for times of less than 2 hours 17 minutes in the 1982 London marathon: KO74 is Merv Brameld of Invicta, KO41 Derek Stevens of Hastings

In 1978 only four men in the world had run the marathon faster than 2 hours and 11 minutes and only three women had bettered 2 hours and 40 minutes. By 1979 this figure had doubled for men and more than quadrupled for women. By the end of 1981, twelve men had broken 2 hours and 11 minutes and an incredible twenty-nine women were faster than 2 hours and 40 minutes.

In 1981 in the UK there were at least 54 marathon races involving something like 40,000 runners. By 1982, these figures had almost doubled, to 106 races with almost 100,000 entrants. In 1980 fewer than 3,000 runners recorded times faster than 4 hours for the marathon; by 1981, 10,000 had run faster than 3 hours and 40 minutes.

The marathon is now not just a supreme test of endurance for the Olympic athlete: women are running marathons, and ordinary men and women are aspiring to finish the 42km — some in what were once regarded as very good times for trained athletes, let alone the ordinary individual.

Whether you have run a marathon, or are going to run one, or would just like to watch or to advise others running one, this book is aimed at increasing your understanding and appreciation of the marathon and of what goes into the preparation for and execution of our greatest and most exciting foot race.

Mark Shearman, who has photographed many marathons, has also run one in under 2 hours 50 minutes

1 The basic physiology of marathon running *Ron Holman*

Success in most athletic pursuits depends upon the production of mechanical work brought about by muscular contractions. In running this mechanical work is utilised within the body to accelerate and decelerate the limbs.

A muscle can be regarded as an engine which obtains its energy essentially from the 'burning' of fuel. Its performance, or capacity for work, depends on both the nature and the availability of the source of energy. In the case of a man-made engine the energy source is easily identified and the engine's energy requirement almost as easily measured: it is simply the rate of consumption of the supplied fuel. The muscle is, however, more complex: it uses several different fuels, and even regenerates some of them itself.

The most immediate sources of energy for a muscle's activity are substances within the muscle called 'phosphagens'. Unfortunately, although these substances are an extremely powerful energy source, there is no really appreciable store of them in muscle, and therefore there is a need for their continual resynthesis. They can be supplemented in two different ways: (1) the combustion of food (measured by the consumption of oxygen); and (2) glycolysis, which is the breakdown of glycogen stored in the muscle and results in the formation of lactic acid. Lactic acid produced in the second of these reactions may be reconstituted to glycogen by means of the first — that is, by an input of energy from food combustion.

So two of our three energy-releasing mechanisms take place without the use of oxygen; they are therefore termed 'anaerobic'. The first of these, the direct use of the muscle's phosphagens, is labelled 'alactic' since no lactic acid is produced; while the second, glycolysis, which involves lactate production, is called a 'lactic anaerobic' (lactacid) reaction.

How do we know which of these mechanisms the muscles will use? Basically the choice depends on two factors: the intensity of the exercise and the duration of the exercise. If the intensity of the exercise is high then it is likely that one of the anaerobic reactions will be taking place; if the exercise is of short duration and fast then it will almost certainly be the first, alactic, mechanism. This is the primary energy source in the so-called explosive athletic events such as shot-putting, long jumping, or the short sprints. It

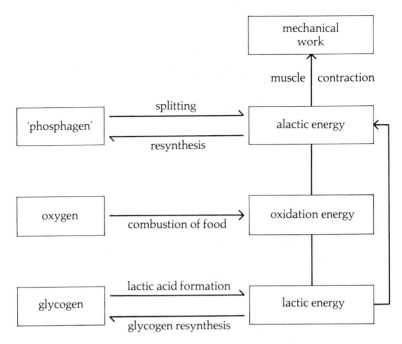

Fig 1. Energy-releasing mechanisms during exercise

reaches its maximum intervention in energy provision over a period of work between three and fifteen seconds long.

However, as we have observed, because of the low amount of phosphagen stored in muscle, should the exercise continue at a high level of work — as for example in the 400m — then the lactic mechanism takes over, reaching its maximum contribution between one and two minutes of work. After about three to five minutes of physical activity, the respiratory processes develop fully and energy provision becomes more aerobic.

We can see, therefore, that in the middle-distance events all three energy-releasing mechanisms may be operating simultaneously but at different intensity levels at different stages of the event.

In the marathon, however, the speed of running may be safely described in physiological terms as moderate, and energy expenditure is largely aerobic. Thus the oxygen demand of the event is below the runner's maximum aerobic capacity, and oxygen consumption during the run itself will therefore be of paramount importance.

Endurance

It is an often observed dictum that 'good sprinters are born and not made'. In recent years, since the advent of muscle biopsy techniques, this statement may be applied also to distance runners. It is clear from the results of scientific research that the end of the athletic spectrum — speed or endurance — at which one excels is largely determined by one's muscle fibres and their percentage composition.

Muscle fibres can broadly be classified into two types, fast-twitch and slow-twitch (FT and ST), although a third type, fast-oxidative-glycolytic (FOG) has more recently been identified. (FT fibres are sometimes termed 'white' and ST fibres 'red'.) The relative percentages of these fibres present in one's muscles are genetically predetermined before birth (although training can affect their cross-sectional area, and certain biochemical changes can occur in both fast- and slow-twitch fibres following training). World-class endurance athletes, such as marathon runners, show a preponderance of slow-twitch fibres — those which are responsible for aerobic (with oxygen) respiration within the muscle cell.

Typically, good distance runners possess over 70 per cent ST fibres and marathon runners often more than 80 per cent: both Frank Shorter and Bill Rodgers have been put in this category, while Alberto Salazar, currently the world's fastest at the marathon distance with 2:08.13, has been reported as having an even higher percentage. On the other hand, Don Kardong, fourth in the 1976 Olympic marathon in 2:11.16, just three seconds behind the third-place finisher Karel Lismont, was known to have only about 50 per cent ST fibres, which types him more as a middle-distance track runner. Later tests proved Kardong's fibres contained exceptionally high levels of oxidative enzymes.

Thus marathon athletes demonstrate a remarkable ability to function aerobically at the highest level; that is, they can run at very high speeds for

Alberto Salazar, here leading in the 1982 World Cross-Country in Rome, has a very high proportion of ST fibres

prolonged periods of time without entering into the realms of anaerobic respiration (oxygen debt), where the appearance of lactic acid as a by-product inevitably results in painful side-effects.

The primary requirement for endurance is that the muscle fibres themselves enhance the level of oxidative enzymes within the cell, thereby enabling large amounts of oxygen to be utilised. It follows, therefore, that there must

Fig 2. The oxygen and carbon-dioxide transport system

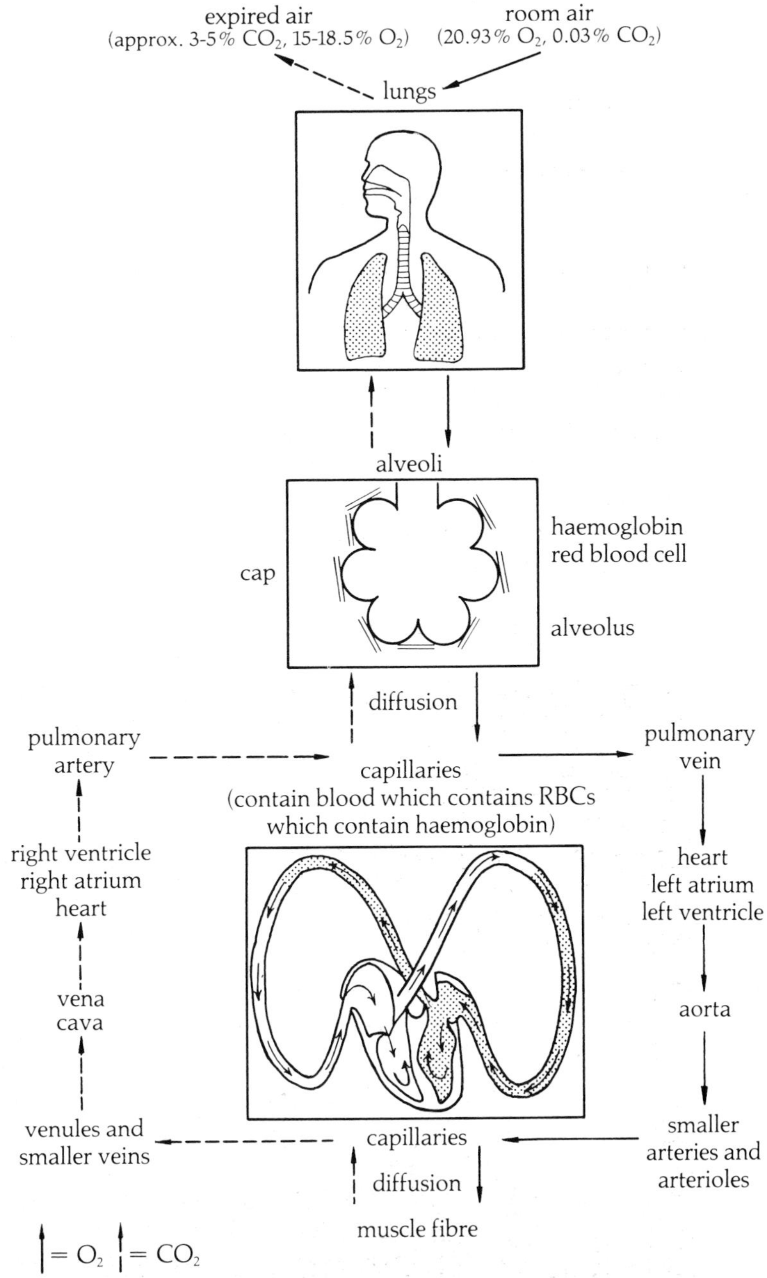

expired air
(approx. 3-5% CO_2, 15-18.5% O_2)   room air
(20.93% O_2, 0.03% CO_2)

lungs

alveoli

cap

haemoglobin
red blood cell

alveolus

diffusion

pulmonary
artery

capillaries
(contain blood which contains RBCs
which contain haemoglobin)

pulmonary
vein

right ventricle
right atrium
heart

heart
left atrium
left ventricle

vena
cava

aorta

venules and
smaller veins

capillaries

smaller
arteries and
arterioles

diffusion

muscle fibre

$\uparrow = O_2$ $\downharpoonleft\!\!\upharpoonright = CO_2$

also be a concurrent increase in the body's capacity both to take in and to transport this oxygen before its consumption within the muscle itself.

Air is moved in and out of the lungs as a result of the action of the respiratory muscles, which expand and contract to create pressure gradients between the lungs' alveoli and the external atmosphere. Ventilation, the flow of air into the lungs, comes about as a result of the diaphragm and chest wall moving to increase the volume of the chest and thereby decrease the pressure within to a level lower than atmospheric pressure.

The main function of ventilation is to optimise the composition of the alveolar gas, which can be thought of as a 'compartment' of gas lying between the air sucked in from the atmosphere and the blood in the alveolar capillaries. The blood in the capillaries continually removes oxygen from the alveolar gas and, by way of exchange, adds to it carbon dioxide, most of which has been formed as a result of the body's metabolic processes.

Certainly training affects lung function: the rate of respiration slows down and, at a given work-rate, the volume of air breathed in is smaller, indicating that the lungs are extracting more oxygen from each litre of air that is breathed in. The chest muscles are undoubtedly strengthened; this is indicated by an increase in 'vital capacity', which is a measure of the maximum volume that can be expelled from the lungs by a forced effort after a maximum inhalation. Trained athletes can have a vital capacity almost 20 per cent greater than that of an untrained individual of similar age and circumstances — and probably even more when the figure is calculated in relation to body size, since marathon runners tend to be smaller than most. The endurance of these muscles increases, too, and this is reflected in an increase in the maximum volume of air that the person can breathe in one minute: a trained runner can generally breathe out 50 to 60 per cent more air in a given time than can the average individual.

The oxygen absorbed into the capillary blood is then transported around the body by the pumping action of the heart. The quantity of blood flowing around the circulatory system (the 'cardiac output') can be defined as the quantity of blood ejected from the heart during each beat (the 'stroke volume') multiplied by the heart rate, and is generally expressed in millilitres (ml) per minute. A typical cardiac output for an average man at rest would be in the range 5,000–8,000ml (8.9–14 Imperial pints; 10.6–16.9 US pints) per minute.

Responses to endurance training are found in both the heart and the general blood circulation. There is an increase in total blood volume; the heart enlarges (cardiac hypertrophy), mainly by increasing the size of its ventricular cavities; and the main arteries enlarge and more capillaries open up to accommodate the increased blood flow.

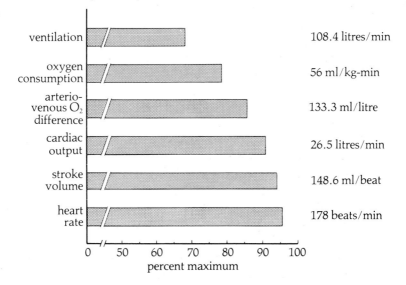

2 HR, 26 MIN, 30 SEC MARATHON PERFORMANCE

ventilation	108.4 litres/min
oxygen consumption	56 ml/kg-min
arterio-venous O$_2$ difference	133.3 ml/litre
cardiac output	26.5 litres/min
stroke volume	148.6 ml/beat
heart rate	178 beats/min

Since marathon runners sweat profusely during training and racing, and also because they are usually smaller and thinner than their sedentary counterparts, they can function with a reduced blood flow to the skin because, by sweating, they dissipate their body heat more efficiently. This adds to the improved efficiency of the circulation, since more blood can be directed to the muscles. Moreover, there is more oxygen in the system: a well trained runner extracts almost 85 per cent of the available oxygen during maximum effort, whereas the untrained individual is unlikely to be able to extract more than about 70 per cent.

Although the cardiac output does not appear to change much in response to training, the slower heart rate both at rest and during a standard work performance is compensated for by an increase in stroke volume. During exercise, in marathon runners this can reach as much as two and a half times the norm for an untrained person.

Overall, then, we can see that a marathon runner possesses not only very efficient muscles but also an extremely powerful cardio-pulmonary system (heart-lung circuit) linked to a very effective peripheral blood circulation. It is not for nothing that more than one exercise physiologist has advised would-be champions to 'choose their parents carefully'. However, training can compensate for very many deficiencies within the human machine.

Maximum oxygen uptake

We can see that a major factor in successful marathon running is the maximum amount of oxygen capable of being transported and utilised by the working muscles: this is known as the 'maximum oxygen uptake' or '$\dot{V}O_2$ max'. Various authorities have stated that training can increase the individual's $\dot{V}O_2$ max by as much as $20-30$ per cent initially, especially if he or she was originally grossly overweight. It should be realised, however, that if the individual is over the age of about 20 and of normal weight then the increase in $\dot{V}O_2$ max will be considerably less than this, probably at most in the region of 10 per cent.

$\dot{V}O_2$ max values are usually obtained by having the athlete run on a treadmill and measuring the amount of oxygen his or her body processes by collecting the respired gas and analysing it for oxygen and carbon-dioxide concentrations. Most top-class marathon runners show $\dot{V}O_2$ max values of over 70ml per kilogram per minute. This is high, but nevertheless rather lower than the usual figures obtained for front-line track distance runners. For example, David Costill (Director of the Human Performance Laboratory at Ball State University, Indiana, USA) has measured Frank Shorter's maximum oxygen uptake as just over 71ml/kg/min, whereas the late Steve Prefontaine

Two athletes — left, Jeff Norman, former fell-running champion and 2:12 marathon runner; and right, Bernie Ford, one of the greatest British cross-country runners of all time, and a 2:10 marathon runner — being physiologically tested in the human performance laboratory at Carnegie School of PE, Leeds Polytechnic

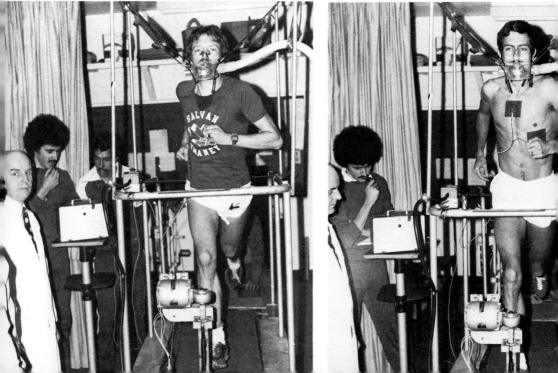

(1972 Olympic 5,000m finalist) had a value of over 84ml/kg/min. These figures can be compared with those obtained from professional soccer players, which are generally in the region of 50—60ml/kg/min.

As Costill himself has pointed out, rather than the maximum value itself, which has been calculated to be over 90 per cent genetically determined, the really important factor is the percentage of that maximum at which an individual can perform while accumulating only relatively low lactic-acid levels.

Thus Derek Clayton, whose maximum value was actually below 70ml/kg/min, could nevertheless operate comfortably at between 86—90 per cent of this value. Similar figures were found for Frank Shorter, and this undoubtedly places these competitors at a possible advantage over those whose maximum values are higher, but who can use only a lower percentage of their $\dot{V}O_2$ max. The percentage obtainable appears also to be more susceptible to the adaptations brought about by training than is the maximum value. The differences may well be due in part to a running action which is more efficient in terms of energy expenditure and thus of oxygen consumption.

Fig 4. Marathon runners are between 5 and 10 per cent more efficient than other distance runners in terms of the amount of oxygen they require to run a given distance

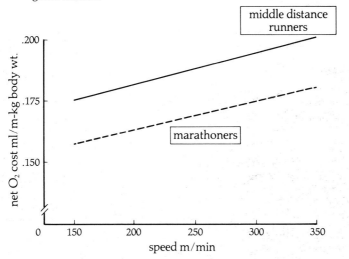

How long do the effects of training on cardio-respiratory fitness last? Accepting that the maximum oxygen uptake is a good potential index of this fitness, we can demonstrate that the advantages of good cardio-respiratory fitness can last well into late middle-age. With the advent of 'masters'' competitions in the USA (known as 'veterans'' events in the UK) scientists have had an even older active population to study, and recent observations have shown that endurance training strongly counteracts the normal ageing effects even after the age of 60.

The advantages of good cardio-respiratory fitness can last well into late middle-age. Endurance training strongly counteracts ageing, even in the over 60s

It can be seen from Fig. 5 that marathon runners probably have an initial genetic advantage, and it is likely that it is for exactly this reason that they are drawn to the event. However, the gradient of the line representing the uptake values of 'normally active' men is steeper than that for the marathon runners, representing a more rapid decline in these values with increasing age. This is probably due to the effects of training adaptations among the runners.

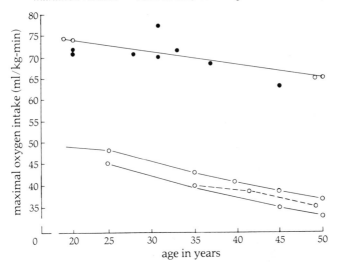

Fig 5. Relationship between age and maximal oxygen consumption (data for marathon runners — solid circles; normally active men — open circles)

The heart

'Fitness' has been described as one of the most misused — and overused — words in the English language. Obviously fitness for sport or work has both an absolute and a relative meaning. The man or woman who can run the fastest, jump the highest, lift the heaviest weights or attain the highest output during a working day must be the most fit for that particular activity. However, when the word 'fitness' is applied in a health programme, for instance, it takes on another meaning. Here it becomes a relative term: for example, a fit, small person may not be able to compete in weight-lifting with a less fit but larger person. If their job is to shovel coal, the smaller person's maximum work output may well be much less than that of his or her bigger counterpart. Obviously, then, fitness is both specific for a task and also multi-faceted, composed of differing standards of neuromuscular coordination, muscle strength, flexibility, anaerobic power, aerobic power (circulo-respiratory endurance) and agility.

Professor Erling Asmussen of the University of Copenhagen has stated: 'As aerobic power undeniably depends on the fitness of the heart, it has attracted great interest because of its use as an indicator of health in relation to coronary heart disease.' Coronary heart disease is the biggest single killer in Western civilisation. The Registrar General's Statistical Review of 1967 showed that, compared with 1950—52, the increase in deaths in the UK from atherosclerotic (arteriosclerotic) heart disease had risen by about 60 per cent.

The percentage of deaths attributable to heart disease which specifically involved coronary arteries was also calculated for various ten-year age groups. In the age group 40−49, the increase for males was from 14 per cent in 1951 to 33 per cent in 1967; and for females from 3 per cent in 1951 to 7 per cent in 1967. The same review showed that during this time period (1951−67) deaths from coronary disease between the ages of 45 and 55 increased from 59 per cent to 81 per cent of the total deaths due to diseases of the circulatory system.

Between 1974 and 1975 in the UK there were over 475,000 deaths from all causes of which over 30 per cent were attributable to heart disease. To this figure can be added a further 15 per cent of deaths from cerebrovascular accidents (brain haemorrhages or thromboses), so that, all told, conditions related to atherosclerosis (hardening of the arteries) accounted for 45 per cent of the total deaths. This compares with approximately 3 per cent attributable to all types of accidents (home and traffic); it should be noted, too, that no particular cancer accounted for more than 2 per cent of the total mortalities.

In the USSR in 1978, data from the Central Statistical Board indicated that 51 per cent of total deaths were from cardiovascular diseases, as compared with 14 per cent from all known tumours including cancer. In the USA in 1972 it was estimated that the annual death toll from coronary heart disease was approximately 600,000.

The way in which coronary heart disease affects its victims was well understood by the mid-1960s. From thousands of autopsy specimens it was known that the three coronary arteries which provide the heart muscle with its blood supply could become largely blocked because of a thickening of their inner lining. This has the effect of starving the heart muscle of oxygen, and can give rise to the condition called angina pectoris, which causes severe pain in the chest. If a blood clot forms in one of these partially blocked arteries then the oxygen lack becomes even more marked, and part of the heart muscle may actually die — a myocardial infarction.

During the 1970s the World Health Organisation published a list of some forty conditions associated (or thought to be associated) with the appearance of clinically manifest coronary heart disease. Dr T. Strasser, the Medical Officer for Cardiovascular Disease for the WHO, has more recently rationalised these factors. He concluded that there are five major primary risk factors which are both uncontroversial and amenable to control: diet and lipids, high blood pressure, cigarette smoking, oral contraceptives, and physical inactivity.

Although cardiovascular disease remains the number one cause of death in the USA, the figure there has declined by 30 per cent in the last fifteen years, as opposed to a decrease of only 17 per cent in the rest of the world. A massive

Fig 6. Coronary risk factors

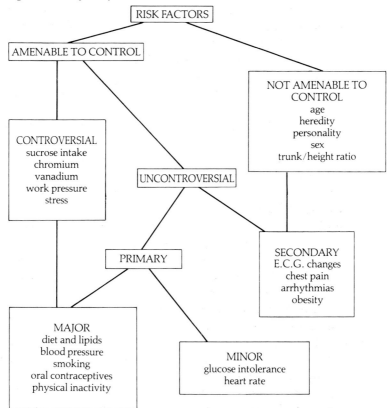

study recently carried out in Rochester, Minnesota, gave a rough indication of the situation in the USA as a whole (although the trend in mortality rates was about 20 per cent lower). It showed that the annual age-adjusted death rate was 142 per 10,000 population in 1960, peaked at 184 in 1969, and steadily declined to 113 in 1978. Although this decline was evident in all age groups it was most noticeable in those aged 30−59 — the 'heart attack years'.

It is difficult if not impossible to specify the reasons for this decline, but G. H. Hartnung and A. M. Gotho believe that dietary changes, lowering of blood cholesterol levels, and the great enthusiasm for running and other forms of exercise are contributory factors. It has been estimated that there are now twenty million joggers in the USA, in addition to probably another twelve million competitive marathon runners.

Medical interest in the effects of marathon running on health almost certainly began with the death of the US runner Clarence De Mar in 1958,

The undesirable aftermath of some of the USA's 12 million competitive marathon runners

aged 69. De Mar's running career spanned almost half a century, during which time he ran in thirty-four Boston marathons, winning seven times and fifteen times finishing in the top ten. An autopsy revealed after his death (from cancer) that his heart was slightly enlarged — as is the case with most endurance athletes — and that his coronary arteries were approximately two and a half times the normal size. Although there was some degree of atherosclerosis, it was far less than had been regarded as normal for a man of his years.

In 1973, Dr J. N. Morris and co-workers published their study of UK Civil Servants and their leisure-time activities. Morris hypothesised that, because work in advanced societies is becoming increasingly light and sedentary, any future contribution to public health would have to come from exercise taken in leisure time. He pointed out that there was evidence from several countries that men in physically active occupations derived some protection against coronary heart disease. The conclusions of Morris's study were that, in men who were participating in vigorous exercise, the risk of developing coronary heart disease was about one third that in comparable men who were not. In men who indulged in a great deal of vigorous exercise the risk was even less.

Morris and his colleagues studied over 16,000 male executive-grade civil servants between the ages of 40 and 64. In the USA R. S. Paffenbarger and W. E. Hale reached similar conclusions in their findings on over 6,000 longshoremen between 35 and 75 years of age.

In the early 1970s a US physician, Dr Thomas Bassler, went so far as to say that when the level of rigorous exercise is raised high enough, the protection [against coronary heart disease] appears to be absolute'. This assertion provoked much controversy, and opponents of Bassler's view began citing as evidence sudden deaths during and after marathon races. However, Dr Ernst Jokl, an internationally recognised authority on sports medicine, searched the world literature and collected a series of 76 cases of sudden death during physical exertion. His conclusions were that in each case there was a reasonable pathological explanation of death, and that it was likely that these deaths would have occurred anyway, possibly even during a sedentary state. Paul Milvy, an epidemiologist from New York's Mount Sinai School of Medicine, thought that, until a longitudinal study of possibly several thousand marathon runners was carried out for a number of years, with a carefully selected matched control group, no really valid conclusions could be drawn.

Nonetheless, H. Sanne carried out a major training study in Gothenburg during 1968−70 involving almost 300 post-infarction patients. Half of his patients underwent physical training of an endurance type and the other half acted as a control group. One year after the infarction (after nine months of training), tests proved that the exercising group had a greater physical work capacity than the resting group, and had increased their maximum aerobic power by 17 per cent — which is approximately the same amount as healthy subjects after similar training. Mortality was significantly higher in the control group two years after the original infarction. E. Varnauskas and his associates demonstrated similar findings in a shorter study carried out over four to six weeks.

In the USA, Stanford University recently mounted a massive heart-disease prevention programme, involving the education of the population about the need for a good, low-cholesterol, weight-reducing diet, less smoking, and sufficient exercise. The university claimed that the programme reached 45,000 people and resulted in a 25 per cent reduction in the incidence of coronary heart disease. If the same programme were to be applied to the population of the UK it would, all other things being equal, be able to achieve a reduction of about 100,000 cases of heart disease per year.

In short, a sedentary lifestyle has been strongly implicated, if not established, as a risk factor for coronary heart disease. Although the evidence to date is not conclusive, it has led to widespread interest in programmes for the improvement of physical fitness which, among other things, may prove beneficial in both the primary and the secondary prevention of coronary heart disease. Marathon running and the training programmes relevant to it may be regarded in such a light.

Marathon runners in the World Veterans Championship 1982

Running for your life

If we examine once more the major primary risk factors listed by Strasser we can make some pertinent observations with regard to marathon runners.

In April, 1982, an *ad hoc* working party in the UK published its recommendations on the prevention of coronary heart disease. One of these was a reduction in the fat contribution to energy requirements — the decrease in fat consumption being offset by an increase in foods rich in complex carbohydrates, particularly bread, vegetables, potatoes and fruit. Such foods are common energy sources among marathon runners (see Chapter 4), and a diet based largely on them has the added benefit of being high in dietary fibre. An increase in fibre intake was recommended recently by the US National Academy of Sciences in its report on the prevention of intestinal cancer to the National Cancer Institute. Of course, it is important — as in all dietary regimes — to ensure that the overall calorie intake does not exceed the energy output.

The plasma level of high-density lipoprotein (HDL) has been shown to be inversely related to the risk of acquiring coronary heart disease. Subjects with existing clinical ischaemic heart disease have lower levels of HDL than healthy subjects within the same community; and it has been proposed that a reduction in plasma HDL concentration may accelerate the development of atherosclerosis, and hence ischaemic heart disease, by impairing the efficiency of the clearance of cholesterol from the arterial walls.

Many scientists have explored the possibilities of an association between an increase in HDL levels and physical activity. Hartnung and Gotho concluded that the high levels found in marathon runners were related to the distances they ran rather than to their diet. The work of Dr Peter Wood at Stanford University supports these views, but he adds the guarded rider that such studies may be biased as a result of a self-selection effect. He pointed out that, in his own studies, it was easier to persuade those with an initially higher HDL level to run longer distances, and that levels did not change until a threshold exercise level — 10 miles (16km) per week — was maintained for at least nine months. He observed also that fitness increased and percentage body fat decreased sooner and at lower exercise levels than those required for HDL changes.

Varnauskas' study in 1966 was one of several which demonstrated that blood pressure was reduced slightly after training. Others have found that even moderate reduction of overweight may, through lowering the blood pressure, reduce the risk of heart disease.

Smoking is regarded as a particularly important risk factor, especially in those under the age of 50. A survey in a district of Moscow showed that 10 per cent of boys aged 12 to 13 smoke, and for boys a year older the figure is 30 per cent, which is approaching that for smokers among the adult population. Remembering the established links between heart disease and smoking, it is a sobering thought that over half of the 2,545,600 deaths in the USSR in 1978 were from cardiovascular diseases.

Perhaps even more sobering is the knowledge that in the UK the grant awarded to the Health Education Council has been increased for 1982−3 by £2 million to £8½ million. At the same time, there has been a £200 million increase in revenue from tobacco sales to a staggering total of £3,500 million. It has been estimated that it costs the National Health Service £150 million per year to treat smoking-related diseases.

One of the secondary risk factors for cardiovascular diseases listed by Strasser was obesity. This is a major health problem in industrialised nations. Between the ages of 20 and 74, in the USA, over 20 per cent of women and nearly 15 per cent of men are 20 per cent or more overweight. Contrary to popular opinion, this obesity does not appear to be related to affluence, since a large proportion of sufferers have incomes which are below the poverty level. The prevalence of excessive overweight seems to have increased also among people between the ages of 25 and 44 in the ten-year period between 1961 and 1971. In London 40 per cent of the people in a middle-aged sample were found to be obese. In Sweden 50 per cent of men and 70 per cent of women aged 50−60 years were found to be 20 per cent overweight.

Many of the biochemical, physiological and mortality hazards of obesity are associated with or even cause disease. Diabetes mellitus (when contracted in adulthood), arthritis, gout, hypertension and atherosclerosis are all either contributed to by obesity or correlated with it. W. N. Hubbard has calculated that the average life expectancy in the USA could be increased by at least seven years if all obese individuals could be brought down to ideal weight. By way of comparison, the prevention and/or cure of all types of cancer would increase average life expectancy by only two to three years.

A body fat content of less than 10−15 per cent is ideal for men whose weight is around 60kg (132 lb); for women the fat content is approximately 5 per cent higher. Many people have two or three times this amount, and G. A. Bray has remarked that it is not uncommon to find people over 40 whose percentage of body fat is as high as that of the whale!

The size and (possibly) the number of the fat cells in the body are determined by the energy balance — that is, the balance between eating behaviour, metabolic rate and physical activity. With regard to the last of these, although it has not been fully established that inactivity is a cause of obesity, the two are frequently associated.

Of course, the promotion of health through exercise has its opponents, some of whom are members of the medical profession. Exercise cannot simply cancel out all sloth, overeating and bad habits: it should not be thought of in the same way as a pill or a penance which can simply negate self-indulgence. Those who have not exercised for years should begin gently, and we would accept that there are some who should not begin at all.

Even some of the researchers who express caution have acknowledged, however, that the completion of 'vigorous bouts of exertion' brings a feeling of well-being. Professor Lesley Rees of St Bartholomew's Hospital, London, has found increases in natural opiates in the brains of runners, which may provide at least a partial explanation. At London University Professor Lindford Rees firmly believes that running can make a person more alert and

To complete a vigorous bout of exertion makes you feel good

less stressful. In the USA Dr O. Appenzeller found increased beta endorphins in trained distance runners, and postulated that these produced the euphoria sometimes described as 'runner's high'.

There can be little doubt that running can, and often does, reduce emotional tension and stress. As David Levin of Harvard Medical School has stated, 'few challenges in life are so clear-cut or amenable to such immediate gratification'.

Support from family and friends boosts one's emotional satisfaction in this stress-reducing activity

Perhaps the last word should be left to Paul Milvy, who points out the substantial statistical risk from the two factors of weight and cigarette consumption alone on the general US male population. Almost to a man (or woman), marathon runners do not smoke and are very thin (and, moreover, drink little alcohol). The average sub-three-hour marathoner aged less than 35 years weighs in pounds about twice the numerical measure of his height in inches (in kilograms, a little over one third of the height in centimetres): this is about 15 to 20 per cent less than average. Older marathon runners, although slightly heavier, may well be proportionally even lighter than people of similar age in the general population. Thus at least two very important risk factors in coronary heart disease are almost totally absent in virtually all marathon runners.

2 Marathon training *John Humphreys*

Many people who enter marathon races are simply not fit enough. Indeed, it is not unknown when screening even fully trained marathon runners to find someone with a physical abnormality, such as a diseased heart, which renders strenuous endurance activity extremely inadvisable. In some of the big 'people's marathons', often several thousand competitors can be seen walking after only the first few kilometres, and so one has to assume that they are insufficiently fit to run the whole distance.

The aim of this chapter is to provide you with the information that will enable you to be fit enough to run a full marathon. Even if you have already done one year's training, it is probably a good idea to train for the best part of a further year before entering your first marathon race: ideally, after you have run it, you should be fresh enough to drive yourself home, if necessary,

It is important to stress that in training you should always operate within your own capacity. You must appreciate that, although you may feel all right during your exercise sessions, it is possible that you may have some physical abnormality. For this and other reasons it is *essential* that you have a thorough medical examination — preferably before you even start training. The purpose of the examination is to give your physician sufficient information for him to decide at what level — if at all — you should commence your exercise programme. It should include a chest examination, a blood-pressure determination, and a general ears, eyes, nose and throat inspection. In addition, you should be asked to complete a medical-history questionnaire covering your personal and family history of coronary heart disease and the associated risk factors, present medication and treatment, eating and diet habits, smoking history, and current physical activity pattern.

If possible, intending runners should have a complete physical examination, including a 12-lead resting and exercise ECG and blood lipid tests, prior to starting the training programme. The two sets of tests mentioned are particularly applicable if you are over 35 years of age and considered a high risk for coronary heart disease. Low-risk people are those with no relevant symptoms — such as chest discomfort or shortness of breath — and who are under 35 years of age, have no previous history of coronary heart disease and no known primary risk factors that are associated with it (high blood pressure, excessive blood fats and sugar, smoking, obesity and adverse family history). In addition to the medical examination, a fitness evaluation is also desirable, but this is obviously not practicable for the majority of runners.

It is recommended that, if you are under 35 years of age, you should have a follow up examination every two years. For people who are between 35 and 40 this interval should be reduced to 18 months, and after you are 40 years of age the examination should be annual.

Because long-term research into marathon running is lacking, we recommend that teenagers should wait until they are 18 years old before running a marathon.

Finally, it should be appreciated that some individuals ought not to be undertaking any strenuous physical exercise at all. A list of conditions which may either preclude exercise or call for extreme caution is given in Table 1. Only your doctor is in a position to evaluate these 'contra-indications' to exercise, but you should ensure that you read the list carefully.

Reasons for temporarily reducing or deferring physical activities such as running can be seen in Table 2 (page 47).

Table 1 *Contra-indications for strenuous exercise*

1 CONTRA-INDICATIONS	DESCRIPTION*
1 Acute myocardial infarction	A recent heart attack in which a portion of the heart has died
2 Unstable or at-rest angina pectoris	Severe chest pains (sometimes spreading to the arms and up the neck)
3 Dangerous arrhythmias (ventricular tachycardia or any rhythm significantly compromising cardiac function)	Dangerous abnormal rhythms of the heart
4 History suggesting excessive medication effects	Diuretics (agents which increase the flow of urine), psychotropic agents (antidepressant drugs), digitalis (commonly used drug which strengthens the heart resulting in a much slower exercise and resting heart rate)
5 Manifest circulatory insufficiency	Congestive heart failure
6 Severe aortic stenosis	The valves in the opening from the left ventricle to the aorta are calcified (hardened) and constricted, thus severely narrowing the opening

* In consultation with David Hammond, M.D., formerly of Ithaca College, New York, USA

7 Severe left ventricular outflow tract obstructive disease (IHSS)	Disease of the aortic valve
8 Suspected or known dissecting aneurysm	Progressive dilation and destruction of a blood vessel wall
9 Active or suspected myocarditis or cardiomyopathy (within the past year)	Myocarditis = inflammation of the muscle tissue of the heart. Cardiomyopathy = disease of the heart, sometimes resulting in a flabby heart which contracts poorly.
10 Thrombophlebitis — known or suspected	Inflammation of the veins with clot formation
11 Recent embolism, systemic or pulmonary	Obstruction of a blood vessel by a travelling blood clot or matter
12 Recent or active infectious episodes (including upper respiratory infections)	
13 High dose of phenothiazine agents	Tranquillizing drugs and drugs used for other purposes such as lowering blood pressure

2 RELATIVE CONTRA-INDICATIONS

1 Uncontrolled or high-rate supra-ventricular arrhythmias	Irregular heart rhythm
2 Repetitive or frequent ventricular ectopic activity	An abnormal electrocardiogram
3 Untreated severe systemic or pulmonary hypertension	Untreated high blood pressure, in the system or in the lungs
4 Ventricular aneurysm	A blood-filled sac formed by the dilation or expansion of part of an artery
5 Moderate aortic stenosis	See number 1.6
6 Severe myocardial obstructive syndromes (subvalvular, muscular or membranous obstructions)	Disease of the mitral or aortic valve resulting in a failure of the left ventricle
7 Marked cardiac enlargement	Increase in size and thickness of ventricular walls without accompanying collateral circulation
8 Uncontrolled metabolic disease (diabetes, thyrotoxicosis, myxedema)	
9 Toxemia or complications of pregnancy	A pathological condition occurring in pregnant women characterised by the presence in the blood of certain toxic products

3 CONDITIONS REQUIRING SPECIAL CONSIDERATION AND/OR PRECAUTIONS

1 Conduction disturbances
  a Complete atrioventricular block
  b Left bundle branch block
  c Wolff-Parkinson-White anomaly or syndrome
  d Lown-Ganong-Levine syndrome
  e Bifascicular block (with or without 1st° block)

  Abnormalities in the electrocardiogram

2 Controlled arrhythmias

  Abnormal heart rhythm treated by medication

3 Fixed rate pacemaker

  Presence of an artificial pacemaker which programmes the function of a normal heart in fixing the normal resting rate of heart contractions

4 Mitral valve prolapse (click-murmur) syndrome

  A defectively operating heart valve

5 Angina pectoris and other manifestations of coronary insufficiency

  Severe chest pains (sometimes spreading to the arms and up the neck) which become worse with any type of physical work

6 Certain medications
  a Digitalis, diuretics, psychotropic drugs

  See 1.4

  b Beta-blocking and drugs of related action

  Beta-blocking drugs used to slow the heart rate

  c Nitrates

  Drugs used to dilate coronary arteries

  d Antihypertensive drugs

  Drugs used to lower blood pressure

7 Electrolyte disturbance

  Not maintaining the correct balance between the different elements in the body tissues and fluids

8 Clinically severe hypertension (diastolic above 110, grade III retinopathy)

  High blood pressure

9 Cyanotic heart disease

  Failure of blood oxygenation process resulting in a lack of oxygen to the body

10 Intermittent or fixed right-to-left shunt

  Congenital heart disease where the blood goes through a hole from right to left; therefore oxygenation in the blood is low and the individual often turns blue

11 Severe anaemia (haemoglobin below 10 gm/dl)	Decrease in red blood cells, haemoglobin or both
12 Marked obesity (20 per cent above optimum body weight)	Over 20 per cent body fat
13 Renal, hepatic and other metabolic insufficiency	Abnormalities of such organs as the kidney or liver
14 Overt psychoneurotic disturbances requiring therapy	Certain types of mental illness
15 Neuromuscular, musculoskeletal, orthopaedic, or arthritic disorders which would prevent activity	
16 Moderate to severe pulmonary disease	Disease of the lungs
17 Intermittent claudication	Blood vessels of the leg go into spasm or become narrowed; the blood flow is diminished resulting in severe pain in the legs
18 Diabetes	

Table 2 *Reasons for temporarily reducing or deferring physical exercise*

Intercurrent illness — febrile (high-temperature) afflictions, injury, gastro-intestinal
    illnesses
Progression of cardiac diseases
Orthopaedic problems
Emotional turmoil
Severe sunburn
Hangover
Cerebral dysfunction — e.g., dizziness, vertigo
Sodium retention — oedema (swelling), weight-gain
Dehydration
Environmental factors*
    Weather — excessive heat or cold
    Air pollution — smog, carbon monoxide
Over-indulgence
    Large, heavy meal less than two hours previously
    Excessive sex
    Coffee,† tea, coke (xanthines and other stimulating beverages)
Drugs, decongestants, bronchodilators, atropine, weight reducers (anorectics)

---

* You may of course have to *race* in adverse conditions, but you should avoid
  training in them wherever possible. See also Chapter 3.
† Drinking strong coffee in large amounts daily is not to be recommended, despite
  the comments on page 116.

Principles of training

In many respects we are only as active as our heart will allow. The human body, including the heart, is ideally built for physical activity, but to work efficiently it needs to be trained. Long ago it was essential to be able to run just in order to survive, but these days transportation has largely taken over, and many people have now become inactive and consequently prone to a variety of ailments of which heart disease is one of the most serious. As we have seen, in many respects we still have to run for our lives.

Before we discuss training principles, you must understand that if you have been inactive for a number of years — or in some cases merely months — you should not start your exercise programme off by running, and you will need a long period of 'gentler' training before you can begin serious running. We shall come back to this point later. For the aspiring marathon runner, the most important structures to train are undoubtedly the heart and the circulation, and one of the best ways to do this is by the act of running itself. But an untrained person should train slowly — in many cases initially by walking — for several weeks or even months before being ready to run.

OVERLOAD PRINCIPLE

To improve physiological efficiency in response to training a specific exercise overload must be applied. This means that, in a progressive manner, you need to increase the *intensity*, the *duration* or the *frequency* of training. In the case of marathon running the major emphasis should be placed on duration, but obviously applied in a progressive manner. In simplest terms, an unfit person may commence a walking programme which lasts for several weeks, then practise alternate walking and jogging for a further period, then jog continuously, and finally advance to continuous slow running. Each type of training needs to be for a sufficient period of time, to allow the body to adapt to the increased stress.

As you progress through each phase of your training you will be increasing the intensity as well as the duration. You need, however, to keep in mind the fact that generally the highest-intensity training is the most fatiguing, and that therefore initially you should place more emphasis on low-intensity training coupled with low to medium duration. If you increase the intensity too rapidly fatigue will result, and this will affect your future training loads.

Another thing to remember is that, the fitter you become, the more work it will take to improve your level of fitness yet further. There is a limit to the fitness training effect, and the rate and magnitude of the increase varies from one individual to the next. In other words, owing to hereditary differences, some individuals can get fitter sooner and with less training than others. The older you get (particularly above the age of 50) the less trainable you become; in other words, you may have to train on a more regular basis than a younger individual to obtain a similar training response. Also, as you become older, it would appear that you do not retain the fitness gains you have made for so long after the cessation of training. However, it is interesting to note that even elderly people can derive definite benefits from training.

It cannot be emphasised too strongly that any progression in training should be *gradual*, and training must be performed on a regular basis. We shall return to the topic of the frequency with which you should train.

SPECIFICITY OF TRAINING

If you intend to run a marathon, then, although supplementary programmes such as flexibility and strength exercises will help, the most important gains will be achieved by running. You need to include as far as possible in training the specific exercises that will be involved in your ultimate aim — the marathon. This race is essentially an aerobic (or circulorespiratory) endurance event, and so you need to train your aerobic or oxygen transport system using the most appropriate methods of running training.

Although female runners generally train at lower intensities and durations than do males, it is our firm belief that the two sexes should adopt similar training techniques. There exists no conclusive scientific or medical evidence that long-distance running is ruled out for the healthy, trained female athlete — indeed, some female marathon runners, such as Joyce Smith, are capable of better performances than many good male club runners! Most research indicates that men and women adapt to exercise training in a similar manner.

Before we discuss the many types of training methods available it is worth looking at the American College of Sports Medicine's recommendations, as given in Table 3, for the quantity and quality of training for developing and maintaining cardiorespiratory fitness and body composition in the healthy adult. Obviously the guidelines in Table 3 are only for healthy adults, and the length of time you actually run will depend on how fit you are. Remember that *running* is the best form of training for running performances. Once you are sufficiently fit to run a marathon with safety then, even should you injure yourself, some of the activities listed in section 4 of the table — such as swimming and cycling — may be possible, depending on your type of injury. (See also page 80.)

Table 3 *Recommendations for training*

1 Frequency of training: 3 to 5 days per week
2 Intensity of training: 60−90 per cent maximum heart-rate reserve, or 50−85 per cent of maximum oxygen uptake ($\dot{V}O_2$ max)
3 Duration of training: 15−60 minutes of continuous aerobic activity — lower-intensity activity should be conducted over a longer period of time. Because of the importance of the 'total fitness' effect and the fact that it is more readily attained in longer-duration programmes, and because of the potential hazards and compliance problems associated with high-intensity activity, lower- to moderate-intensity activity of longer duration is recommended for the nonathletic adult
4 Mode of activity: any activity that uses large muscle groups, that can be maintained continuously, and is rhythmical and aerobic in nature; e.g., running-jogging, walking-hiking, swimming, skating, bicycling, rowing, cross-country skiing, rope-skipping, and various endurance-game activities

HEART RATE

Although the resting heart rate may range from 50 to 100 beats per minute, the higher your endurance capacity the lower your resting heart rate will generally be. It is a good idea to record your heart rate for the ten seconds immediately following exercise: multiply this by six to convert it to beats per minute. The heart rate in the first ten seconds after a bout of exercise will be almost identical to what it was during the time you were exercising. Periodically, each week, you may find it useful to record your heart rate following a run and note the decrease as you become fitter. Obviously, to make a fair comparison, you have to undertake a similar exercise task.

It is also worthwhile to take your cardiac recovery index following some of your exercise periods. Using a standard test of your choice, such as a 6km run (provided you are fit enough to do this!), record your heart rate for ten seconds immediately afterwards, preferably from the radial (wrist) artery, and then multiply by six, as above. During the recovery period, record your heart rate again for ten seconds between one minute fifty seconds and two minutes, and then multiply by six. Subtract the latter heart rate from the former, and you have your cardiac recovery index (CRI). As you get fitter, your CRI will be higher because you are returning to the resting state faster.

For example, following a 2km run your heart rate over the first ten seconds is, say, twenty-five. Multiply by six to convert to beats per minute:
$$25 \times 6 = 150$$
However, your heart rate over the ten seconds between one minute fifty seconds and two minutes is only fifteen. Again, multiply by six to convert to beats per minute:
$$15 \times 6 = 90$$
Your CRI is therefore 150−90; that is, 60.

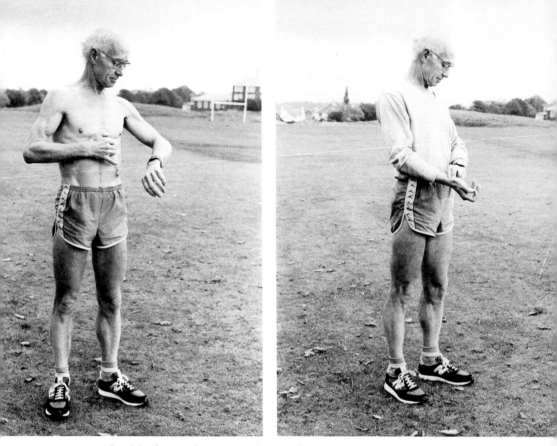

Eric Marsh started running at the age of 59, and two years later ran a marathon in 3 hours 33 minutes; he has beaten several ex-international veteran runners. Here he records his heart rate (left) in the heart region itself, and (right) from the radial artery

As you become fitter over your months of training you will notice, too, that your heart rate is lower during your exercise. Basically, this is because the exercise task is not taxing your body to the same extent as before.

It is a good idea also to record your breathing and heart rates in bed ten minutes after you have awakened, and to note the decrease in both as your level of fitness improves. They may be recorded over a full minute. Remember that your breathing rate is the in-and-out movement of your chest, and can be observed just below the diaphragm. As you become fitter, your breathing rate becomes lower because your metabolism is becoming more efficient.

Finally, each morning following urination record your weight. It should, once you are fully fit, remain relatively constant. Remember, however, that if you select one of the predominantly carbohydrate diets (see page 108) your weight will usually increase by perhaps a kilogram or two.

Running training

Many types of running training are suitable preparation for the marathon. Remember that it is important to do both continuous training and interval training as part of your build-up.

The theoretical basis of all *interval* training is that, when short rest periods are interspersed between periods of heavy exercise, more work can be achieved overall. For example, if instead of running at a fast continuous pace for twenty minutes you run for five minutes and then rest for five minutes, etc., you will probably be able to achieve at least three times the total amount of work. (Shorter work and rest intervals — e.g., 30 seconds' running, 30 seconds' resting — at the same intensity would be less fatiguing, but would not stress the oxidative capacity of the muscles to the same extent as do the longer five-minute intervals.)

Moreover, because interval training involves periodic rest periods, the total stress on your system is less, and therefore *slow interval* training can be used in your build-up to continuous types of running. If you are improving your aerobic or oxygen transport system by interval running, it is very important that you do not run the intervals too fast, and also that only relatively brief recoveries should be taken between each interval: obviously the recovery periods can be shortened when you are fit enough to benefit from this type of training. Although there is a place for endurance interval training it should not form the major part of your training.

The most effective form of training for improving your central oxygen transport system (including heart and lungs) is by *continuous* running involving as large a muscle mass as possible. Continuous running should form the major part of your training. You need also to establish the right balance between your continuous and interval training methods; the training schedules on pages 62 — 72 will give you guidance on this.

In deciding on running methods, we suggest you study the following list. We will advise you later at what stage to introduce these methods into your training.

O   long, slow continuous running
O   medium-paced continuous running
O   alternating fast and slow continuous running
O   fast continuous running
O   interval running (endurance or aerobic)
O   interval running (aerobic and anaerobic simultaneously)
O   repetition running
O   fartlek, or speed play

○   hill running
○   jogging
○   anaerobic training (not recommended for most runners)

Long, slow continuous running refers to running comparatively long distances at a comfortable slow pace, although one that is in excess of jogging speeds. During this type of running the muscles are working aerobically (i.e., with oxygen — see Chapter 1), and your heart rate will be approximately 130−150 beats per minute (BPM). You will be working at only about 50−70 per cent of your maximum oxygen uptake ($\dot{V}O_2$ max). Finally, your breathing response should be reasonably comfortable: you should not be gasping for breath.

Medium-paced continuous running is a compromise between long, slow distance running and fast continuous running. Your heart rate will be approximately 140−160 BPM and you will be using approximately 55−75 per cent of your $\dot{V}O_2$ max. Although you will be breathing more frequently and in greater depth than during long, slow continuous running, once again you should not be gasping for breath and you should be able to talk while running.

Alternating fast and slow continuous running is where the first mile is run at a fast continuous pace (e.g., in six minutes), followed by an easier second mile (e.g. in seven minutes), then by another fast mile, and so on. (If you are practising on a track, this is roughly equivalent to covering the first 2,000m in seven and a half minutes, the next 2,000m in nine minutes, and so on.) This is hard training, and should be undertaken only when you are fully endurance-trained. Obviously, in the example given, you are averaging about six and a half minutes to the mile, which is a reasonable pace for a longer distance: you should select the distance you want to cover carefully, bearing in mind your own level of fitness. This type of running can be a preparation for fast continuous running.

Fast continuous running is probably the hardest type of training and should be done only when you are fully fit, and even then only in relatively small amounts because of the fatigue which you will encounter. With this sort of running the heart rate is approximately 160−180 BPM, more white or fast-twitch fibres in your legs are involved (see page 26), and you would be using 70−90 per cent of your $\dot{V}O_2$ max.

Interval running (endurance or aerobic) is where comparatively short distances are run — for example, 400m at approximately 70−80 per cent of your top speed over the distance — with comparatively short recovery periods of about one minute in between runs. Naturally, the fitter you are, the shorter the recovery periods can be. However, you must not run the repetitions at full speed as this would involve your *anaerobic* system, which is not required in normal marathon races. Several possible ways of training using this method are shown on page 63.

Interval running to develop aerobic and anaerobic power simultaneously (speed + endurance) involves the intervals being run at about 85 − 95 per cent of your top speed over the training distance, but with longer recovery times being taken between the intervals; you may either walk or jog slowly during the recoveries. If you are a normal marathon runner, you need undergo only a limited amount of this type of training (examples of suitable practice regimes can be seen on page 72). As with interval running for the aerobic system, you should gradually increase the number of intervals you can do. Do not do more intervals than you can achieve without slowing drastically.

Repetition running differs from interval training in terms of both the length of the interval run and the duration of the recovery time between intervals. It involves repetitions of longer distances with, after each, a period allowing almost complete recovery (usually by walking), during which the heart rate drops to well below 120 BPM. The repetitions may be one to two miles (1.6 − 3.2km) long, and should be run at a fast pace to duplicate the stress encountered under racing conditions. As the pace is higher than in fast continuous running, you should usually do only a few repetitions. You can use this type of training as a preparation for fast continuous running.

Fartlek, or *speed play*, is an informal type of training consisting of alternate fast and slow running; it is considered 'unscientific' in the context of true interval training. Essentially, you combine slow continuous running, medium-paced running, interval running, hill running, fast continuous running, sprinting and walking, generally without involving any rigid structure in terms of intervals, running rates and recoveries. Nevertheless, fartlek can give you a reasonably hard and satisfying workout, and one that you can enjoy doing in pleasant surroundings. This type of training is preferably done over natural surfaces such as golf courses, grass, or in woods, where varying and uneven ground can be encountered. It allows for a certain freedom from highly structured workouts; and many world-class marathon runners find it a refreshing change from these.

Hill running can be done in two ways: either you run a series of repetition sprints up a hill with recovery periods in between; or you can select a course containing several varying hills and run it on a continuous circuit. By doing the latter type of training you are able to use a large percentage of your VO_2 max as you run uphill, something which would be more difficult to achieve while running on the flat. You obviously need to be fully fit before you go in for this type of training, and even then you should take care to introduce it in the right amount. You will find it strengthens your legs as well as your heart and lungs.

Jogging is really a form of very slow running in which you normally place only minimal stress on your heart-lung circuit. You may be exercising at a heart rate of 100 – 120 BPM, and you should have no difficulty in holding a conversation as you go along. It acts as a good prerequisite or aerobic base before normal

Eric Marsh demonstrates a relaxed running action while hill running. Note his relaxed neck muscles

running is undertaken, and you may find it beneficial also in the training week following your first marathon. Obviously it does not elicit the same training response as running does, but millions of people find it a very enjoyable pastime.

Anaerobic training is not recommended for the normal marathoner, although a very limited amount of it may be incorporated in the training schedules of top-level runners as preparation for fast starts and surges in competitive marathons.

Table 4 *Some physiological differences between fast and slow continuous running**

FAST CONTINUOUS RUNNING	SLOW CONTINUOUS RUNNING
1 Heart rate 160−180 BPM approx.	Heart rate 130−150 BPM approx.
2 Neurologically more related to the demands of racing	Neurologically less related to the demands of racing
3 High involvement of fast-twitch (white) fibres	High involvement of slow-twitch (red) fibres
4 High percentage of $\dot{V}O_2$ max used (70−90 per cent)	Low percentage of $\dot{V}O_2$ max used (50−70 per cent)
5 Lactates relatively high	Lactates relatively low
6 More involvement of LA/O_2 energy system; i.e., speed and endurance combined	Muscles working essentially aerobically; i.e., with oxygen
7 Possibly greater effect in improving the stroke volume (amount of blood ejected per beat from heart)	More efficient sweat rate for a given blood flow
8 Helps to improve the percentage of $\dot{V}O_2$ max a runner can use during running and training	Does not improve the percentage of $\dot{V}O_2$ max to the same extent as does fast continuous running
9 Too much of this can lead to fatigue and a breakdown in training	A high mileage can be obtained by this type of training
10 Causes a bradycardia effect (lowering of heart rate at rest)	Causes a pronounced bradycardia effect (lowering of heart rate at rest)
11 Relatively heavy stress-load placed on the muscles, ligaments and tendons	Results in decreased circulatory stress during the performance of submaximal exercise

* Obviously medium-paced running will involve some of these training responses to a greater or lesser degree

Warm-up and cool-down

The amount of warm-up you do depends upon your age, level of fitness and the environmental conditions you are about to encounter. Before you undertake any training or racing you should prepare your system for action by several minutes' jogging, at a progressively increasing pace, and then follow this by a range of specific flexibility exercises (see page 73). On a very hot or humid day you may in general spend less time warming up, whereas in cold windy conditions you should definitely go through a full warm-up. During the first 200—300m of jogging, run flat-footed in order not to put too much strain on your achilles tendon.

You should not warm up to the extent of sweating. On a very cold day you may find you can keep your track suit on, whereas on a warm day this will not be necessary. We recommend that, prior to a marathon race, you warm up 15 to 20 minutes before the event, allowing five minutes of light walking before you actually start to race.

Why is it necessary to warm your body before activity? Research indicates that a whole-body warm-up which raises muscle and blood temperatures can significantly improve athletic performances. Warming up is important for preventing muscle soreness or injury, and to protect the heart from ischaemic changes (shortage of blood) that may otherwise occur during sudden strenuous exercise.

Cooling down after strenuous exercise is extremely important for physiological reasons. If you do not do a cool-down, venous return of blood to the heart — which has been largely driven by the muscle pump — drops too abruptly so that blood pooling may occur in the extremities. This can result in shock, or at least in hyperventilation (elevated breathing rate), which causes lower levels of carbon dioxide and muscle cramps. If you are returning to your home, club or wherever following a run, slow up several hundred metres from your destination and jog slowly, eventually dropping to a brisk walk and then to ordinary walking pace. The total cool-down period should be approximately five to ten minutes.

Running schedules (first-year cycle)

OVERWEIGHT?

It must be appreciated that many people are simply not fit to run through being overweight. If it is not possible to have your body fat accurately measured, we recommend you assess the extent of any overweight by referring to Table 5: ideally, you should fall within the ranges shown in the table.

Table 5 *Desirable weights*
weight in pounds,* according to frame, in indoor clothing

MEN AGED 25 AND OVER

height	frame			height
feet/inches	small	medium	large	metres
5 2	128−134	131−141	138−150	1.57
5 3	130−136	133−143	140−153	1.60
5 4	132−138	135−145	142−156	1.63
5 5	134−140	137−148	144−160	1.65
5 6	136−142	139−151	146−164	1.68
5 7	138−145	142−154	149−168	1.70
5 8	140−148	145−157	152−172	1.73
5 9	142−151	148−160	155−176	1.75
5 10	144−154	151−163	158−180	1.78
5 11	146−157	154−166	161−184	1.80
6 0	149−160	157−170	164−188	1.83
6 1	152−164	160−174	168−192	1.85
6 2	155−168	164−178	172−197	1.88
6 3	158−172	167−182	176−202	1.90
6 4	162−176	171−187	181−207	1.93

WOMEN AGED 25 AND OVER†

height	frame			height
feet/inches	small	medium	large	metres
4 10	102−111	109−121	118−131	1.47
4 11	103−113	111−123	120−134	1.50
5 0	104−115	113−126	122−137	1.52
5 1	106−118	115−129	125−140	1.55
5 2	108−121	118−132	128−143	1.57
5 3	111−124	121−135	131−147	1.60
5 4	114−127	124−138	134−151	1.63
5 5	117−130	127−141	137−155	1.65
5 6	120−133	130−144	140−159	1.68
5 7	123−136	133−147	143−163	1.70
5 8	126−139	136−150	146−167	1.73
5 9	129−142	139−153	149−170	1.75
5 10	132−145	142−156	152−173	1.78
5 11	135−148	145−159	155−176	1.80
6 0	138−151	148−162	158−179	1.83

* To convert pounds to kilograms, divide by 2.2
† For women between 18 and 25, subtract 1 pound for each year under 25

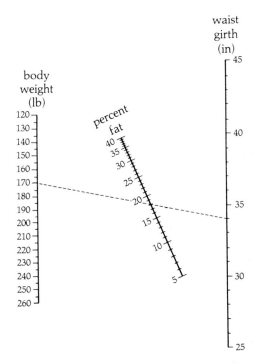

Fig 7. Prediction of relative body fat in men from waist girth and body weight

In addition, you may like to refer to Fig. 7 to estimate the percentage of body fat you possess. Just take a ruler from your body weight in pounds to your waist girth in inches and read off the percentage of fat on the scale in the centre. When measuring your waist girth hold the tape-measure horizontal at the level of the umbilicus. (Unfortunately this nomogram is for men only: a similar chart for women is not available.)

If you are a male with less than 19 per cent fat or a female with less than 22 per cent, jogging should not be too dangerous. Once you have got well into your running programme this level will probably drop to 15 per cent, in the case of a man, and 18 per cent in that of a woman.

A third method of assessing the extent of any overweight is to stand nude in front of a full-length mirror, both sideways and face-on, and note if you have any bulges of fat, particularly around the waist area. When standing face-on to the mirror, extend your body, lifting yourself up and down on your toes (which should remain in contact with the floor). If you have excess fat it will clearly be seen to bounce up and down.

If you are excessively overweight (i.e., weigh over fifty pounds more than the maximum weight listed for your sex, height and frame in Table 5), it would be worth your while following the progressive walking programme for the extremely overweight individual as given in Table 6; this programme should be used in conjunction with a diet, preferably one drawn up by your doctor.

If you are twenty pounds or more over the relevant weight given in Table 5, you are recommended to train by walking for at least eight weeks before you start your jogging programme. Construct your own schedule similar to the one in Table 6, but progress through it more swiftly, according to your capacity, walking initially four days a week and then five after the first three weeks.

If possible, do your initial walking on soft ground — for example, on the grassy outskirts of your local golf course.

Table 6 *Progressive walking programme for the excessively overweight individual* (to be used in conjunction with dieting)*

Week	Distance (miles)	Time goal (min)	Times per week
1	2.0	40½	3
2	2.0	39	3
3	2.0	38	4
4	2.0	37	4
5	2.0	36	5
6	2.0	35	5
7	2.5	45	5
8	2.5	43	5
9	3.0	52	5
10	3.0	51	5
11	3.0	50	5
12	3.0	49	5
13	3.0	48	5
14	3.0	47	5
15	3.0	46	5
16	3.0	45	4

* At least fifty pounds above the maximum weight listed according to sex and height in Table 5, page 58.

INITIAL JOGGING AND RUNNING PROGRAMMES (BLOCK 1)

It is obviously impossible to indicate a starting point for training which will suit everyone but, if you have passed your medical examination and are not excessively overweight, we suggest you progress initially by the following methods.

O   jogging and walking alternately
then
O   jogging continuously
then
O   slow interval running, taking relatively long recoveries, plus jogging
then
O   slow continuous running over relatively short distances, progressively
    built up by increasing duration and intensity each week

If you have not done any regular exercise for six months or more, we suggest
you spend at least six months doing this type of training before progressing to
a more strenuous regime. The object of this training is for you to develop a
good endurance or aerobic training base. If, however, you have been running
four or five times a week for five or six months, you may commence the running programme with block 2 (page 63).

Guidelines in following the first jogging and running programmes are as
follows:

1   Spend the first month jogging and walking alternately — e.g., jog
    300m, walk 100m, then repeat . . .
2   Work within your fitness level, each week gradually increasing the
    jogging and decreasing the walking.
3   Each week gradually increase the total mileage you cover: a 5 per cent
    increase per week is acceptable.
4   Attempt each week to increase *gradually* the intensity or speed at
    which you exercise.
5   Maintain the same speed for a full training week before you make any
    attempt to increase it further.
6   If you find yourself feeling particularly tired during training, reduce
    your speed of running rather than the distance you cover.
7   Attempt to cover the same distance daily, although in the first few
    weeks of your programme you may decide to have a relatively hard
    day followed by a light day — e.g., 5km covered on Tuesday but only
    2km on Wednesday, both distances run at the same speed.
8   Do not try and rush the programme! You can spend at least six
    months on this initial part of your training. Progress to slow
    continuous running only when you are capable of running without
    gasping for air. You should be able to hold a conversation while
    running, and should not feel shattered at the end of the run.
9   During this preparation period try to run on soft level ground as much
    as possible.

10   During the slow interval training, it is suggested you do only two or
     three sessions per week, but you should include also two jogging
     sessions per week.
11   With the endurance interval training sessions run short distances —
     e.g., 300m — reasonably fast, and allow yourself a relatively brief
     recovery period, depending upon how fit you are. (The shorter the
     recovery period, the greater the endurance or aerobic training effect.)
        The total period of time you spend on each type of training
     during your initial training cycle will depend partly on hereditary
     factors and partly on how you respond to the training. The time
     phases shown in Table 7 may give you a useful guide for your initial
     training programme.

Table 7 *Initial training programme*

Cycle	Type of training	Time spent	Sessions per week
A	jogging and walking alternately	1 month	minimum 3 maximum 5
B	jogging continuously	2 months	minimum 4 maximum 5
C	slow interval running and jogging	1 month	minimum 2 maximum 3 + 3 jogging sessions
D	slow continuous running	2 months	minimum 5 maximum 6

12   Get a good night's sleep — the increased activity will result in your
     requiring more sleep. 'Early to bed' is the keynote.
13   Make sure you purchase a good shoe with a wedge heel. The uppers
     must be able to 'breathe', as the build-up of heat in the shoe will
     otherwise produce blisters. Break in new shoes gradually — and *never*
     in a race.
14   Wear the correct clothing for the weather — where possible cotton, as
     this helps to prevent friction. The application of vaseline can help to
     avoid chapped thighs.

A weekly schedule for Table 7's Cycle C might be as follows ('EIT' means
endurance interval training):

Monday	2 miles' (3.2km) jogging
Tuesday	slow EIT: 8 × 300m (40-second recoveries)
Wednesday	2 miles' (3.2km) jogging
Thursday	slow EIT: 6 × 400m (50-second recoveries)
Friday	2 miles' (3.2km) jogging
Saturday	slow EIT: 8 × 300m (40-second recoveries)
Sunday	rest

○ distance covered: jogging   6   miles (9.6km)
                        EIT   4½ miles (7.2km)

                        total   10½ miles (16.8km)

The jogging runs can be undertaken at lunchtime or at any convenient time but, if possible, do them at the same time each day. Note that the EIT exercises, which are good aerobic training, will produce a slightly different training response from that produced by the jogging. You must remember not to run the intervals too fast — approximately 70–80 per cent of your maximum speed over the training distance, if you are fit enough — and to take only short recovery breaks.

Several methods of EIT for Cycle C of Table 7 are given in Table 8. In each case, you should do only the number of repetitions for which you can maintain the speed at which you ran the first distance. If, for example, you find yourself running the sixth repetition considerably more slowly than you ran the previous ones, then end your training session for that day.

Table 8 *Endurance interval training methods*

Length of run	Type of recovery	Length of recovery
200m	slow jogging	20 seconds
300m	slow jogging	40 seconds
400m	slow jogging	60 seconds
500m	walk first 100m, then jog slowly for the remainder	80 seconds
600m	walk first 100m, then jog slowly for the remainder	90 seconds

RUNNING PROGRAMMES (BLOCK 2)

Having successfully completed your first six months of training you are now ready to introduce rather more variety into your programme. You can start some of the following running methods.

○ medium-paced continuous running
○ alternate fast and slow continuous running
○ repetition running
○ fartlek

In addition, you can carry on with long, slow continuous running and endurance interval running. The time phases shown in Table 9 may be followed.

Table 9 *First-year training: block 2*

Type of training	Time spent	Sessions per week
medium-paced running	6 months	2
alternate fast and slow continuous running	6 months	1 (alternate weeks)
repetition running	6 months	1 (alternate weeks)
fartlek	6 months	1 (alternate weeks)
slow continuous running	6 months	4 − 5
interval training (aerobic)	6 months	1 (alternate weeks)

During your second six-month block of training you may introduce, on two days of the week, two training sessions in the same day — but not on consecutive days. This will help to improve your recovery from training, an important part of a marathon runner's preparation. Individuals of either sex who are over 50 years old should train only once per day, and should not indulge in alternate fast and slow continuous running but instead in slow continuous running.

Set out below are examples of three continuous weekly training schedules. Notice that hard days' training are followed by easier ones, and that two daily training sessions have been introduced on both Tuesday and Thursday. The total distance covered per week will, obviously, depend upon the individual, but in all cases the weekly progression should be gradual. Clearly, towards the end of your first year in training, you will be covering a greater distance each week.

Note that a relatively long run — over 6 miles (9.6km) — is undertaken each week; later you should increase this distance by having two long runs per week. Notice, too, that the total distance covered per week is increased only very gradually.

WEEK 1

	morning	afternoon/evening
Monday		3 miles' (4.8km) alternate fast and slow continuous running
Tuesday	2 miles' (3.2km) slow continuous running	2 miles' (3.2km) slow continuous running
Wednesday		3 miles' (4.8km) medium-paced running
Thursday	2 miles' (3.2km) slow continuous running	2 miles' (3.2km) slow continuous running
Friday		3 miles' (4.8km) medium-paced running
Saturday		6 miles' (9.6km) fartlek or repetition running
Sunday		rest

○ distance covered: 23 miles (36.8km)

WEEK 2

	morning	afternoon/evening
Monday		EIT: 12 × 400m (60-second recoveries)
Tuesday	2½ miles' (4km) slow continuous running	2½ miles' (4km) slow continuous running
Wednesday		3¼ miles' (5km) medium-paced running
Thursday	2½ miles' (4km) slow continuous running	2½ miles' (4km) slow continuous running
Friday		3¼ miles' (5km) medium-paced running
Saturday		rest
Sunday		6 miles' (9.6km) slow continuous running

○ distance covered: 25½ miles (40.4km)

WEEK 3

	morning	afternoon/evening
Monday		3¼ miles' (5km) alternate fast and slow continuous running
Tuesday	2¾ miles' (4.4km) slow continuous running	2¾ miles' (4.4km) slow continuous running
Wednesday		3½ miles' (5.6km) medium-paced running
Thursday	repetition running: 2 × 1¼ miles (2km), walk recovery	2½ miles' (4km) slow continuous running
Friday		3½ miles' (5.6km) medium-paced running
Saturday	rest	
Sunday		6¾ miles' (10.8km) slow continuous running

O   distance covered: 27½ miles (44.1km)

Bearing in mind the training guidelines we have given you (see pages 43−60), it should be relatively easy for you to construct your own schedules. In many cases, by the end of the first year you should be running between 40 and 50 miles (64−80km) per week and, more importantly, feeling relatively good on it. Once you have gained a good endurance (aerobic) base it represents a form of capital investment, and you should then be able to get into better physical condition than you have ever been before. But remember, if you are ill — e.g., suffering from an infection — reduce or even desist from training until you are fit to run again (see pages 43−47).

Running schedules (second-year cycle)

When you begin your second-year block of training, it is a good idea to start including some

O   fast continuous running
O   interval running for aerobic and anaerobic power simultaneously (in other words speed and endurance training combined)
O   continuous hill running

The methods of training listed in Table 9 (page 64) will still be a part of your programme, however. The three new cycles or blocks of training described in

66

Table 10 each continue for approximately four months. In each case, reduce the distance you run by approximately 30 per cent every fourth week, and use this fourth week as a recuperation or reduced-work period. In the 3 blocks of training no alternate fast and slow continuous running, interval training (speed and endurance combined) or fast continuous running is recommended for men and women over 50 years of age; these exercises should be replaced by slow continuous running.

Three examples of training weeks are given, one for each block. By following the training guidelines we have already given you (see pages 43 – 57) you should be able to construct your own scientifically based schedule. That *you* should devise it is essential, as obviously individuals react differently to training. Moreover, you are the only person who really knows how you are progressing.

Table 10 *Second-year blocks*

BLOCK 1: DURATION 4 MONTHS

Training done	Approximate number of training sessions per week	Training guidelines
slow continuous running	4 or 5	On 2 days per week train twice a day; still important for recuperation or recovery training; include 1 long run per week
medium-paced running	1	1 session per week of medium-long duration to be maintained
hill running (continuous)	1	1 session in alternate weeks
alternate fast and slow continuous running	1	1 session in alternate weeks
interval training (speed and endurance combined)	1	This type of training now introduced
fartlek	1	1 session in alternate weeks

Notes: One rest day may be taken each week. Hill running should be done continuously over a number of small hills. The total distance per week in this block is 50 – 60 miles (80 – 96km). Both duration and intensity should be slightly increased over earlier training.

SPECIMEN SCHEDULE FROM BLOCK 1

	morning	afternoon/evening
Monday	5 miles' (8km) slow continuous running	Interval training (speed and endurance combined): 4 × 700m, recovery time equal to running time
Tuesday		8 miles' (12.8km) medium-paced running
Wednesday	6 miles' (9.6km) slow continuous running	6 miles' (9.6km) slow continuous running
Thursday		5 miles' (8km) alternate fast and slow continuous running
Friday	5 miles' (8km) slow continuous running	5 miles' (8km) slow continuous running
Saturday		6 miles' (9.6km) hill running (continuous)
Sunday		9 miles' (14.4km) slow continuous running

○   distance covered: about 57 miles (91km)

Note: On those days on which there is a particularly hard training session — i.e., Tuesday, Thursday and Saturday — you should do only the one run.

BLOCK 2: DURATION 4 MONTHS

Training done	Approximate number of training sessions per week	Training guidelines
slow continuous running	5	Include 1 long run per week
medium-paced running	2	Include 1 long run per week
hill running (continuous)	1	1 session every week now introduced
alternate fast and slow continuous running	1	1 session in alternate weeks only, to allow for more medium-paced running in your schedule
fartlek	1	1 session every week now introduced

Notes: On three days per week you should train twice in the day. In this block it is important to get two long runs, one of about 14 miles (22.4km) and the other of about 10 miles (16km), done each week. The total distance per week in this block is 60 – 70 miles (96 – 112km).

SPECIMEN SCHEDULE FROM BLOCK 2

	morning	afternoon/evening
Monday	5 miles' (8km) slow continuous running	7 miles' (11.2km) hill running (continuous)
Tuesday		10 miles' (16km) slow continuous running
Wednesday		6 miles' (9.6km) medium-paced running
Thursday		6 miles' (9.6km) alternate fast and slow continuous running
Friday	4 miles' (6.4km) slow continuous running	4 miles' (6.4km) slow continuous running
Saturday	7 miles' (11.2km) fartlek (light)	8 miles' (12.8km) medium-paced running
Sunday		14 miles' (22.4km) slow continuous running

O distance covered: 71 miles (114km)

Notes: In this block of training the emphasis is on duration, but the runs are done at a slightly faster overall pace. Also in this block one rest day per week is recommended, but this is optional, depending upon how you feel.

BLOCK 3: DURATION 4 MONTHS

Training done	Approximate number of training sessions per week	Training guidelines
slow continuous running	5	This type of training now very important to balance the high-intensity training
medium-paced running	1	This activity now reduced
hill running (continuous)	1	1 session (alternate weeks); reduced owing to introduction of fast continuous running
fast continuous running	2	This type of training introduced *only* if you are under 50 years of age

interval training (speed and endurance combined)	1	Used every week for sharpening-up purposes but *only* if you are under 50 years of age
fartlek	1	Very important to relieve the stress of high-load training

Notes: On three days per week you should train twice in the day. Total distance per week in this block is 70−90 miles (112−144km).

SPECIMEN SCHEDULE FROM BLOCK 3

	morning	afternoon/evening
Monday		7 miles' (11.2km) fast continuous running
Tuesday	2 miles' (3.2km) fartlek	4 miles' (6.4km) slow continuous running
Wednesday	interval training (speed and endurance combined): 6 × 800m, recovery time equal to running time	14 miles' (22.4km) slow continuous running
Thursday		8 miles' (12.8km) medium-paced running
Friday	8 miles' (12.8km) slow continuous running	8 miles' (12.8km) slow continuous running
Saturday		6 miles' (9.6km) fast continuous running
Sunday		18 miles' (28.8km) slow continuous running

○   distance covered: 78 miles (125km)

Notes: In this block you should be training seven days per week. Now that you have completed block 3, you may undertake your first marathon. Notice that in this block of training you train twice on each of three days of the week, while on Wednesday and Sunday long continuous runs are done. On the three days with particularly hard training sessions — i.e., Monday, Thursday and Saturday — only one training run is carried out.

Of course, the three schedules given are only examples of the type of weekly schedule you should be contemplating while training in each of the three blocks: you may be covering less or more distance per week. The important thing is to notice that the training is *balanced*: generally, a hard training day is followed by a lighter day, and the days on which there are two training sessions (if practicable) are well spaced out through the week. Remember particularly that *on no account must the fast continuous runs be run flat out* as this would cause fatigue and affect your training for the succeeding few days.

Before you can even consider running your first marathon you should have been running seventy miles per week for at least six weeks and preferably longer. The most vital thing to remember is that your training load should show a gradual progression over the months, keeping pace with your fitness capacity but never exceeding it.

In your second year of training you may decide to race every five or six weeks. You should initially run short races — i.e., four or five miles (6.4 – 8km). If you do decide to take part in a middle-distance race, you should not undertake any hard runs for at least 72 hours beforehand; consequently, your training load should be reduced overall for that week. Before you race your first marathon it is advisable to have raced one or two 10-mile (16km) races plus a half-marathon or preferably a 15-mile (24km) road race.

For the average marathon runner it is not advisable to race too many marathons. After two years of training, you should run in your third year a maximum of only two marathons, later increasing this to a maximum of three in your fourth year of training. Having had your first taste of marathon racing, you may well decide to run only two per year!

SECOND-YEAR INTERVAL TRAINING

Some examples of interval training (speed and endurance combined) for the second-year blocks are given in Table 11. In each case, the length of the recovery time between runs should be the same as the time you took doing the run. You should be travelling at about 85 – 90 per cent of your maximum speed over the training distance, and should end your session as soon as you find yourself unable to run the distance in roughly the same time as you took at first. Increase the distance only gradually from 700m to 1,100m, spending about three weeks at each distance before progressing to the next. The purpose is to train your oxygen (i.e., endurance) heart-lung circuit and your lactic-acid system.

Table 11 *Examples of interval running for developing speed and endurance combined*

Length of run	Type of recovery
700m	slow jogging
800m	slow jogging
900m	slow jogging
1,000m	walk first 100m, then jog for the remainder of the time allocated
1,100m	walk first 100m, then jog for the remainder of the time allocated

THE MARATHON RACE

When you line up for your first marathon race your main goals are, presumably, to complete the race in a respectable time, and at least to run the full distance! The best advice is not to get carried away at the start: don't run too fast too soon. Try to pace yourself to run at an even speed throughout the race.

Also, do not forget to take environmental conditions into consideration. If it is exceptionally hot or humid run the first few kilometres more slowly than normal, and expect your overall time to be greater. Make sure you prepare yourself properly for racing in such conditions. This topic is dealt with in more detail in Chapter 3.

It is very important after races, particularly long-distance ones such as the marathon, that you allow proper time for your body to recover. If, for example, you have been running 70–80 miles (112–128km) per week up until the penultimate week before the race, then you need to reduce this afterwards to perhaps 20 miles (32km) in the first week and thereafter increase this distance by only 10 miles (16km) per week over the next two to three weeks. During this period we suggest you run only four times per week (slow continuous running). If possible, train on flat, soft ground, such as on the edge of a golf course, as your legs will have taken quite a beating after having run 42km on the hard road. If you do not allow your body to recover properly — and this applies even to world-class athletes — you are likely to suffer from chronic fatigue and, during this period, be more prone to injuries.

Flexibility training

The two important types of supplementary training are flexibility exercises and strength exercises; 'flexibility' refers to the range of movement in the joints and the spine. Most athletic events require a good level of flexibility, and marathon running is no exception. In both active and less active individuals this level can be improved significantly by the correct programme.

The marathon runner needs a reasonable level of flexibility to help him move more efficiently and maintain a relaxed body posture. A certain degree of greater strength should accompany an increased level of flexibility; strength exercises are to be found on pages 76 — 79. Good joint mobility also helps to reduce the aches and pains that are associated with age — moreover, stiff joints are subject to more strain during locomotion than are flexible ones. Slow stretching exercises, such as the ones illustrated, are recommended because the energy cost is lower, fast stretching is more likely to result in muscle soreness, and there is less chance of overextending the various tissues involved. The exercises illustrated are for both male and female runners of all ages.

You need to be reasonably fit before you can start your flexibility programme. Whether your muscles are in a trained or a non-trained state, it is advisable before a session to jog slowly for several minutes until your cardio-respiratory system (heart and lungs) has had long enough to adjust to the demands of the activity, and until the temperature of your body has risen — this is particularly important if you are middle-aged or elderly.

Generally, the more strenuous the exercise period you are going to undertake, the more important your preceding flexibility routine becomes. When doing the flexibility exercises you should breathe naturally as and when required. It is vital to perform the exercises in a slow, controlled manner: bouncing, dynamic stretching movements should be avoided. You should do the flexibility exercises to the point of reasonable discomfort, gradually applying a greater intensity of effort as you become more supple — that is, keeping the movements slow but using greater force. You should think in terms of going through your flexibility routine three or four times per week.

When starting, hold the recommended position for three to four seconds; after six to eight weeks hold it for ten to twelve seconds and do three sets in each position. Continually change from one body position to another. Rest for thirty seconds after one complete set of all the recommended exercises.

You will be pleased to know that, once a good range of flexibility has been achieved, gains are lost only slowly! Ideally we suggest you do your programme immediately before starting a training run; also you should go into your main exercise within twenty or thirty seconds after completing your flexibility routine, so that your body is still warm.

Fig 8. Stretching exercises

1 *Lower leg: to stretch the calf muscles*
Stand with toes on a raised object, hold on for support with arms. Lower heels as far as possible towards the floor, raise and repeat several times (heels at no time actually touch the floor)

2 *Hamstring, groin and back stretch*
From a seated position with the legs stretched as far apart as possible and straight, one of the ankles is held with both hands and the upper part of the body is taken towards the held foot. Repeat holding opposite side

3 *Head rotation*
Stand erect, hands on hips, feet 30–35cm (12–14in) apart. Slowly rotate the head clockwise in a full circle. Repeat but rotate the head in the opposite direction

4 *Hip flexor stretch*
From a position on your back, slowly pull the knee of one limb towards the chest, hands held just below the knee. Repeat with opposite leg

5 *Lower-back stretch*
Lying on the back, holding each leg below the knee, pull both knees up slowly towards the top of the chest and hold

6 *Upper-trunk stretch*
Lying on the stomach, push the upper body back to extend the arms fully. Attempt to keep the pelvis on the floor, and hold head back

7 *Upper-back and shoulder stretch*
Stand with feet 30−35cm (12−14in) apart, with elbows bent but parallel to the ground. Keeping the elbows parallel to the ground slowly pull them back and hold in the stretched position. Relax and then repeat. This exercise helps to correct round upper back

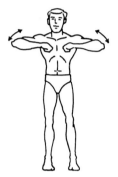

8 *Hamstring stretcher*
Place foot on a chair keeping leg straight. Take your head towards your knee and hold. Change to opposite leg and repeat. (After several weeks use higher chair.) This exercise can also be done while sitting on the floor, legs out in front and together, then forward with head, placing hands between knees

9 *Groin stretch*
Seated and with knees pointed outwards apply gentle pressure pushing down on the knees. Release the position and repeat

10 *Hip and upper back stretcher*
Legs up and over. From a position lying on the back the legs are held straight and pulled over the head until the toes touch the ground. If this is done slowly the hip flexors and abdominal muscles will be strengthened while the hamstrings and back are stretched

11 *Thigh stretch*
In a prone position, reach back with both hands and clasp the ankles. Slowly lift the legs up and off the ground to form a 'cradle' position. Hold in the stretched position for 10 to 12 seconds, relax, and repeat

Strength training

Although a suitable strength programme involving weights or isokinetic equipment will probably improve your running, the vast majority of ordinary marathoners do not have access to such equipment. For this reason, the strength exercises recommended in the following pages do not require the use of weights. Remember to jog for several minutes outside, or run on the spot inside, before you do these exercises.

For the first three months of this programme do only two moderate sessions per week, well spaced out, but increase this to three sessions after the initial period. The number of repetitions and sets you tackle at the start will depend upon your muscular condition, but recommended beginning numbers are given for specific exercises. You may wish to do your strength exercises at a time when you are not going to do a run.

When you reach the fitness level at which you are able to perform large numbers of repetitions of these exercises, you may like to do the exercises in sets. Allow yourself 20 seconds' recovery time between each exercise and 1 minute's recovery time between each set. Remember to shift the concentration from one body region to another — e.g., from legs to arms to abdomen — as you go through the exercises.

Arm and shoulder muscle strengthener (push-up). With your hands outside your shoulders, bend your arms slowly to lower your body until your chest just touches the ground; then return to the original starting position. If your shoulder muscles are weak, this exercise may be done initially with both knees on the ground; but, as your arm and shoulder muscles improve, both knees should be kept off the floor while doing the exercise. Also, if you narrow the distance between both your knees and your hands, with your knees on the floor, the exercise is easier to do; it is a good idea to start the exercise with a narrow base. Do this exercise without pausing. Start with 4 repetitions and each week increase by 2 repetitions. A variation on the push-up is to clap hands while in this semi-prone position; another is to have your feet resting on a bench or chair.

Abdominal strengthener 1. Take up a position lying on your back with your arms by your side and your palms flat on the ground. Keeping your legs straight, raise them until your heels are some four to six inches (10 — 15cm) above the ground. Hold this position momentarily and then lower your legs in a controlled fashion. Once your abdominal muscles are strong enough, you will find you can hold the position for 4 — 6 seconds before lowering your legs. Start with 4 repetitions and gradually build up each week as your strength improves.

Arm and shoulder muscle strengthener

Janet Hartley, a PE student at Carnegie School of PE, Leeds Polytechnic, who recently ran her first marathon in a respectable 3:38, here demonstrates various strength exercises without weights

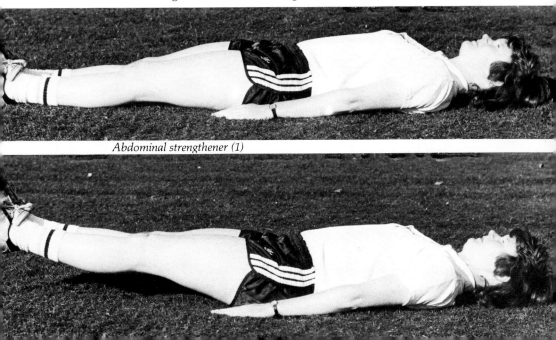

Abdominal strengthener (1)

Abdominal strengthener (2) — sit-up

Squat thrust (burpee)

Squat jump

Lower back strengthener

Abdominal strengthener 2 (sit-up). Lying on your back as before, with the back of the head resting on the floor, raise your head and chest until, with straight arms, you can touch the front of your kneecaps with your fingertips; then return to the starting position. If you cannot touch your kneecaps, then reach forward as far as is comfortable. The back of your knees should be approximately four inches (10cm) off the ground. Do this exercise without pausing. Start with 6 repetitions and, as your strength improves, each week gradually increase the number of repetitions.

Squat thrust (burpee). The squat thrust is an endurance test involving many large muscle groups: rapid shifts of the position of the body are the key. To adopt the initial squat position, place the palms of your hands on the floor beside your feet. Thrust your legs out to the rear, thereby taking up the front-support position: at this point the body must be perfectly straight. Bring your feet back up beside your hands so that you are once again in the squat position; finally, stand up. The aim is to perform as many repetitions as possible within a one-minute period.

Squat jump. This can be used as an alternative to the squat thrust. Stand with your hands on your hips and with one foot a step ahead of the other. Jump into a squat position so that your legs are at a 90-degree angle, and then jump again as high as possible, extending the knees. Change the position of your feet on the way down, so that when you land the foot that was originally ahead of the other is now behind. Then jump again. Start with a few repetitions and gradually build up each week.

Lower back strengthener. Start off by lying face-down with your arms shoulder-width apart and stretched out in front of your body. Raise both your chest and your legs (which should be kept straight) from the floor to adopt a position in which your upper and lower back are arched: raise your legs and chest to the point of moderate discomfort. Hold this position briefly, and then lower yourself back to the starting position. Begin with 4 repetitions, and build up the number over the weeks.

Well developed trunk and abdominal muscles play a significant role in sparing the spine from strain and damage. The spine obviously takes quite a pounding as your feet hit the ground several thousand times on every training run. So remember that well trained abdominal muscles are a must.

So far as leg strength is concerned, the running you are doing as part of your normal training will obviously strengthen your legs to a point, but squat jumps and squat thrusts will give them extra strength. Hill running helps, too, particularly if you are running uphill on soft ground such as sand dunes.

Recommended exercises for the injured

The type of injury you have suffered determines what type of activity you can do. With some leg injuries it is still quite possible to cycle, either on a stationary ergometer or on a normal bike. In many cases swimming is possible: if you can't swim, you can walk relatively quickly through the water (in the shallow end, of course!). Don't forget that, even if you are unable to run, it may be possible for you to do extra strength or flexibility exercises — or both. If you have been relatively inactive for over a week, build up your level of fitness progressively: don't expect to continue where you left off before your injury.

Overtraining

Overtraining is common among new runners. It is simply a result of doing too much too soon, or of not allowing sufficient rest periods after each session of exercise. It can happen to the world-class marathoner as well as to the novice — indeed, everybody falls into the trap of overtraining at some point in their running career.

   If you find it impossible to complete the training distance or to maintain the training pace, then firstly reduce the speed you are running at and secondly, if necessary, the distance you had intended to run. The best protection against overtraining is to build up your training load progressively, and not to be in too much of a hurry. Even athletes of international standard occasionally have to recover either by training lightly for a week or even by taking a complete rest from running. Some of the more common symptoms of overtraining are

○ reduced performance and raised resting heart rate
○ higher breathing rate both at rest and during exercise
○ sore muscles, particularly the thighs (very common)
○ increased tendency to infections — e.g., colds, swollen glands at side of neck
○ increased irritability, impatience and intolerance
○ loss of appetite
○ restless sleep and lethargy
○ stomach disorders — e.g., diarrhoea, constipation
○ anaemia, possibly resulting in headaches and dizziness
○ lack of the desire to train
○ continued gradual loss of weight (i.e., weight lost during exercise is not being replaced as it should be)
○ difficulty in co-ordinating movements while running

Especially if you experience several of these symptoms together, be your own doctor and reduce your training load immediately.

If you experience an abnormal heart action while you are running, such as an irregular pulse, fluttering, pumping or palpitations in the throat or chest, or a very sudden burst of rapid heart beats, stop exercising and consult your doctor as soon as possible. If while exercising you suffer pain or pressure in the middle of the chest or in the arm or throat, then again you should immediately stop exercising and consult your doctor. Finally, if you are light-headed, dizzy or uncoordinated, or if you break out in a cold sweat, go blue or faint, stop exercise immediately. Don't bother with a cool-down: just sit with your head down between your legs until the symptoms pass. *And consult your doctor.*

3 Environmental conditions *Ron Holman*

Heat

Many environmental conditions and changes affect the marathon runner, and of these one of the most serious is heat.

During running, only about 25 per cent of the energy consumed is used for movement; the remaining 75 per cent is converted into heat, and this will often accumulate faster than it can be dissipated. Such internally produced heat is described as intrinsic; the situation is exacerbated if the intrinsic heat is supplemented by extrinsic heat from sources such as the sun.

Since the total energy required to run a marathon is about 4,000 Calories, clearly some 3,000 Calories are converted into waste heat. In fact, it has been estimated that, without any means of heat loss, the body temperature of the average runner would rise by more than 30 Centigrade degrees (86F°) — obviously, this would be fatal several times over!

Heat loss is therefore extremely important. Some excess heat is lost by convection; i.e., through the cooling effects of the wind and the movement of your body through the air. The amount of heat lost in this way clearly depends upon the difference between the temperature of the body and that of the surrounding air, the speed of any wind, and the rate at which the body is travelling.

Any exercise taken in hot conditions will result in blood being diverted to the skin from other parts of the body, so that heat can be lost from the surface by radiation. This reduces the central blood volume and the overall effectiveness of the body's circulation.

Most of the runner's excess heat is dissipated through the mechanism of sweating. As sweat evaporates it subtracts a certain amount of heat from the surface of the body. The rate at which it evaporates, and therefore the rate at which the process can dissipate waste heat, depends to a certain extent upon the rate of air movement over the body's surface.

Sweating inevitably results in a loss of body fluid; the hotter the environment, the greater the loss. During a marathon, this may account for as much as 5 per cent of the runner's body weight. A reduction of this order, it has been calculated, leads to a 20–30 per cent decline in the muscles' work capacity, despite the fact that there is no demonstrable effect on the runner's maximum

Fig 9. Typical heat balance during a marathon race

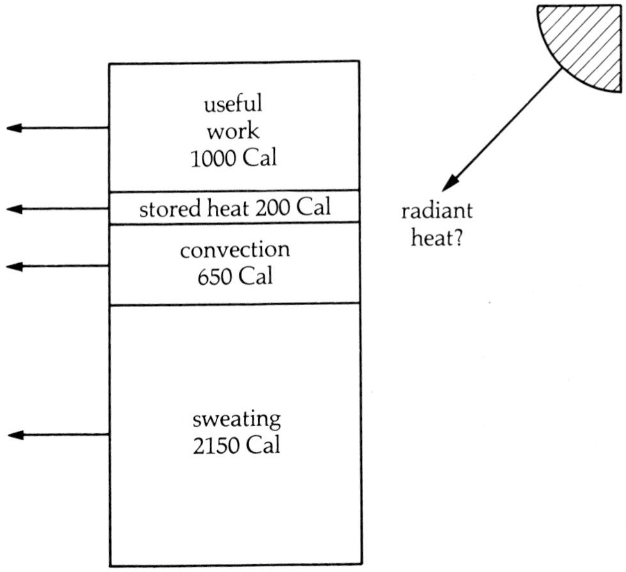

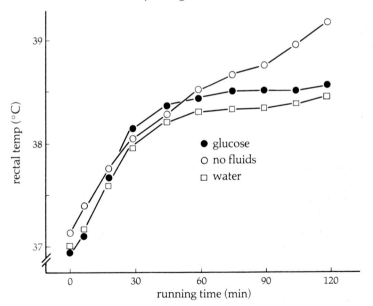

Fig 10. Changes in body temperatures during two hours of treadmill running, with and without fluid ingestion

Regular fluid intake is essential to prevent dehydration

oxygen uptake. If dehydration ever amounted to 10 per cent of the body weight, it is likely that circulatory collapse would occur.

Whenever the external temperature approaches that of the skin — about 35°C, 92°F — loss of heat by convection and radiation more or less ceases, so that sweating is the only means of cooling itself left to the body. Remember that it is the *evaporation* of the sweat that is important: if it merely rolls off you it does no good at all. When the environment is both hot and dry, evaporation occurs freely; but when it is humid — that is, when there is a high concentration of water vapour in the air — the evaporation is impaired. This is why all long-distance runners dread humidity.

Experiments have shown that trained marathoners sweat at a surprisingly uniform rate: the average is around 1.7 litres (3 Imperial pints, 3.6 US pints) per hour, with a further 0.3 litres (10 – 10.5 fl oz) of water lost *via* the lungs each hour. D. L. Costill has observed that, despite the fact that runners may lose 4 – 6kg (8.8 – 13.2 lb) of water during the marathon, few are able to ingest more than 0.3 litres during the race. However, it has been shown that even this partial replacement is effective in reducing the risk of overheating. It should be noted in this context that there is no significant difference in effect between plain water and a glucose solution; the latter is therefore preferable.

If you are going to compete in a marathon in a hot climate it is as well to take certain steps in preparation. This acclimatisation will happen naturally if you arrive ten to fourteen days before the competition and carry out your final training in the ambient climatic conditions. The first few days should be spent in relaxed training, after which you will notice that you are beginning to sweat earlier during your training runs and also that you are sweating more profusely. (Check the dietary advice on salt intake — see page 103.)

You can at least partially acclimatise yourself, even if you cannot afford the luxury of arriving ten or fourteen days before the race, by making a point of training in hot and humid conditions whenever they may obtain in your area. Even if they never do, some experts believe that you can simulate such conditions by, for example, wearing a tracksuit and extra clothing while you train.

Many runners wear hats and T-shirts when it is hot. This is not a good idea: a surprisingly high proportion of body heat is lost from the head, while a T-shirt may prevent sweat evaporation from as much as 40 per cent of your body surface. If you are worried about the possibility of sunburn, then either get yourself a protective tan beforehand or use a suitable ultraviolet-filtering cream during the race.

Wear loose-fitting, thin clothing; light-coloured clothing reflects the sun's radiant heat better than does dark. String vests — especially those cut well from the back area — expose more of the body surface and so help heat loss by both convection and sweat-evaporation; the 'Freedom' shorts manufactured by Ron Hill Sports fulfil the same function in the thigh area.

Be sure to sponge yourself frequently, especially on the face, the back of the neck and the thighs: this aids cooling considerably. Before using the

Cooling water!

Sponge yourself frequently

Squeeze excess water from the sponge

sponge, squeeze any excess water from it; otherwise water may run down onto your shoulders or thighs, encouraging painful chafing from the vest straps and shorts, respectively.

In hot climates, remember to wear light clothing even when you are not training or racing. Make sure that you are drinking plenty of fluid. It is useful to record your body weight daily in the early morning after you have urinated: a loss of weight may indicate a chronic state of dehydration. Look at the urine, too: under normal circumstances it should be a pale lemon colour, and if it is darker than this it may mean that you are not drinking enough. During training and racing, do not assume that thirst will give you adequate warning of excessive dehydration. A man walking in a temperature of 38°C (100°F) with nil humidity loses about 1 litre (1¾ Imperial pints, 2 US pints) of water per hour.

Another point worth remembering in hot climates is not to eat large meals, especially of hot food. It is much better to eat more frequent and regular smaller ones, preferably cold meals such as salads. Well seasoned vegetables and fruit will help with mineral replacement.

In summary, then, you should remember before the race

○ to wear clothing that is light in both colour and texture, and make sure it is not too tight

○ to drink enough before you start running to get you to the first drinks station — 0.3 litres (about half a pint) thirty minutes before the race should be plenty

○ to drink *and* sponge at every opportunity, bearing in mind that, since your thighs are the parts of you that heat up most during running, you will get the greatest cooling effect by sponging them

○ to be practised at getting as much (non-alcoholic) drink inside you as possible

○ to start at a reasonable pace — not one that you have no hope of keeping up for the distance

○ not to warm up: gently stretch and jog if you must, but *not* in a tracksuit

Drink enough before the race begins . . . but not too much!

Be well practised at drinking as much as you can while running

A gentle stretch in light clothing: don't get too warm

After the race — and, indeed, after a training session — setting yourself down in front of an electric fan will help your body to lose heat by convection, and thereby assist heat loss. Over the few days following the race, reduce your training load and increase your intake of carbohydrates. You will find that your recovery time after a marathon run in hot conditions is longer than if you had been running in cooler climes. This is possibly because your muscle fuel, glycogen (see page 108), is used up more rapidly when conditions are hot.

Runners are sometimes taken ill some distance from medical or first-aid assistance, and so it is as well for coaches, helpers and marathon officials to know something of the various heat illnesses. These are summarised in Table 12.

Table 12 *Summary of heat illnesses*

type	symptoms	first-aid care
heat cramps	painful contraction of voluntary muscles	direct pressure; increase fluid and electrolyte intake; rest
heat exhaustion	skin is wet; runner is nauseated, glassy-eyed and tired; pulse is rapid but strong; runner may be unconscious or exhibit cramping	move athlete to cool spot, remove clothing and cool him/her; if rapid improvement not seen seek medical assistance
heat stroke MEDICAL EMERGENCY	skin hot and red and may be dry; runner may not be sweating; pulse rapid but weak; body temperature high (40.5°C, 105°F, or more); respiration shallow and, often, runner unconscious	maintain breathing, cool athlete and seek medical assistance; transport to hospital quickly; hydrate if runner is conscious

Cooling is best carried out by convection — for example, by fanning the runner — and not by covering him or her with cold towels or sponging with cold water.

Cold

Although very few marathons are run in conditions of extreme cold, training goes on all the year round, and so considerable distances may be run in the cold.

The same considerations govern the heat balance of your body whether the environment is hot or cold. In just the same way as when you are running in the heat, the speed of any prevailing wind and of your body through the air is important. The relative movement of the air brings into play what is known as the 'wind chill factor'; for example, a relative wind speed of 16km/h (10mph) will have the effect of reducing a still-air temperature of 17°C (60°F) by 7C° (12.6F°) because of its chilling action.

Several thin layers of clothes are a better insulator than a few thicker layers. A hat, particularly a woolly one, will cut down the heat loss from the head, and gloves will protect the hands. Remember that, even in the cold, you sweat during exercise; sweat-soaked clothes are not good insulators. Synthetic materials are not as good as natural ones; and an outer windproof layer is of paramount importance — as skiers and yachters will testify. Rain suits of various commercial makes are now produced which, when worn over a track suit, are very efficient at keeping out the cold, especially in wet and windy conditions.

Hypothermia is most usually encountered among runners who are both poorly clothed and slow-moving, and who therefore are unable to generate sufficient body heat to counter their heat losses and so maintain their body temperatures. They feel cold, look cyanosed (i.e., their faces and extremities are bluish), have low oral and rectal temperatures, and may suffer from muscle cramping. First-aid treatment involves placing the runners in warm surroundings as soon as possible and giving them hot drinks. Wrapping in warm, dry blankets is helpful; if the runner's clothing is wet, remove it first.

Muscle cramps can best be treated by flexing the adjoining joint so as to stretch the cramping muscle. Often this can be done simply by supporting the runner into a standing position. If the cramps are due to hypothermia, warmth will help alleviate them.

Many runners who train and race through the winter months feel that they have a permanent cold. This is usually a reaction to the cold air causing a slight inflammation of the nasal and respiratory passages, and there is no harm in carrying on running. However, runners should beware in case they have a genuine infection: if there is any evidence of this being so — e.g., a high temperature — all running should cease. Training with such an infection has been known to cause an inflammation of the heart muscle (myocarditis), and has even, in a few reported cases, eventually been fatal.

FOG AND RAIN

There is good evidence that, by contributing to respiratory disease, fog can be a distinct health hazard to the runner. When there is fog about it is far better to miss a few days' outdoor training and instead to do some muscular endurance exercises or running on the spot indoors rather than risk developing a bronchial complaint.

Some runners have experienced difficulties when training in the cold in conditions of high humidity. This should not stop you training but, if you do have problems in such conditions, you should be aware that you will display less than your usual verve.

Running in the rain presents few problems except for the fact that you get wet. Wearing masses of clothing is a bad idea, since the garments simply get heavier and heavier as they get saturated with water. Much better, then, to wear a light rainproof top in addition to your normal gear. Obviously, you should discard wet clothing as soon as possible after your run.

Traffic

At least in the winter months, a great deal of your training will have to be carried out on the roads, and here you are likely to encounter the problem of traffic. Where possible, use the pavement. If you have to run in the road itself, go in the direction facing the oncoming traffic so that you can leap to the side if a driver fails to notice you. (This reverses the usual procedure in a race, which will normally be run in the same direction as the traffic, the organisers having obtained police cooperation.) At night, wear light-coloured, bright clothing — special gear incorporating fluorescent or reflective strips is now available.

If you have chosen a well lit road to run on, another problem may present itself. Well lit roads are almost certainly busy ones. Automobile exhausts produce a gas called carbon monoxide, and this has the unhappy property of being able to attach itself to the haemoglobin in your bloodstream in place of oxygen molecules. Haemoglobin which has been 'caught' by carbon monoxide molecules is unable to transport oxygen to the body tissues, including the muscles; under normal circumstances, the carbon monoxide will be removed naturally from the bloodstream, but this is a slow process (it can take eight hours for 50 per cent of an increased level to be expelled), and until it is complete your muscles will be receiving less than their full quota of oxygen. So it is a good idea to make some effort to find a road that is both well lit and relatively traffic-free.

Incidentally, among its many other disadvantages, smoking, like traffic fumes, has the effect of loading the haemoglobin with carbon monoxide.

Some reports have suggested that taking extra quantities of vitamins C and E can help against pollution, but there seems little evidence to support this. The exercise of running itself helps speed up the excretion of carbon monoxide — but this is not much use if at the same time you are breathing in more of the gas.

One Japanese study has shown that the effects of carbon-monoxide pollution extend more than 20m (65.6ft) outwards from the edge of the road (although another study from the same country showed that even a gentle wind can reduce the concentration by 10 per cent or more, particularly when the levels are between 25 and 35 parts per million). Asher J. Finkel, of the American Medical Association's Department of Environment, Public and Occupational Health, has reported that, whereas normal Los Angeles air contains $10-12$ppm of carbon monoxide, in heavy traffic this is increased to $37-54$ppm: one level measured during a traffic jam was as high as 120ppm.

So, while running along a busy road can often be a convenient and time-saving way of training — for example, you can run to and from work — it does entail a significant exposure to air pollutants which can seriously impair your health. Wherever possible, then, opt for less busy roads or, preferably, parks and woodlands.

Dogs

Dogs may be man's best friend but they can be the running man's worst enemy. There are as many approaches to the problem of hostile or excitable dogs as there are runners. Some people suggest stopping to offer an outstretched hand to be sniffed but, as well as adding nonproductive minutes to your training run, this involves the risk of mangled fingers. Others propose barking back, but once again the success of this technique depends upon the attitude of the canine end of the conversation.

Probably the best idea is simply to ignore the beast or, if necessary, to cross the road and run on the other side. The same technique is recommended should you encounter a specimen of that section of the human race which seems to think it clever to shout facetious remarks at runners.

High altitudes

If you intend to compete or train at altitude, you should know something of its effects. The problems of exercising at altitude have in the past attracted attention mainly because of sporting competitions held in such conditions — e.g., the Pan American and the Olympic Games held in Mexico City, and the soccer World Cup held in Chile.

The uptake of oxygen by the haemoglobin in the blood is influenced by the partial pressure of oxygen in the alveolar air in the lungs at the site of the blood-air gaseous exchange (see page 28). This pressure is itself governed by the ambient atmospheric pressure, which is of course reduced at increased altitude. The net effect is that there is less oxygen available to the runner.

J. A. Faulkner and others found that at an altitude of 2,300m (7,546ft) there was a loss of 13 per cent in maximum oxygen uptake, and at 3,100m

(10,171ft) a loss of 20 per cent. Because of such losses, any given submaximal exercise will utilise a greater proportion of the aerobic capacity. Faulkner found that runs of 3 miles (4.8km) were 2−13 per cent slower in Mexico; and L. G. C. E. Pugh, studying top-class runners over the same distance, found an average deficit of 8.5 per cent which, after four weeks' acclimatisation, was reduced to 5 per cent.

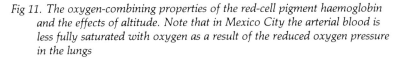

Fig 11. The oxygen-combining properties of the red-cell pigment haemoglobin and the effects of altitude. Note that in Mexico City the arterial blood is less fully saturated with oxygen as a result of the reduced oxygen pressure in the lungs

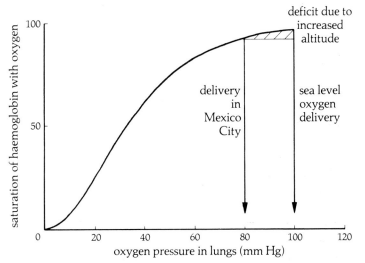

Physiological adaptation to high altitudes involves almost immediate responses in respiration — at first a more rapid breathing rate, then a greater depth of inhalation — and more gradual responses in the nervous, muscular and cardiovascular systems. The best documented acclimatisation response is an increase in the oxygen-carrying capacity of the blood due to increases in the haemoglobin and packed-cell volume: initially this is an acute response, brought about by a reduction in the volume of blood plasma. Some authorities believe that there is also an increase in myoglobin, the oxygen-carrying pigment in the muscles.

There has been much controversy over altitude training. Pugh and J. R. Owen have recommended reduced activity during the first week at altitude, while B. Balke, J. T. Daniels and Faulkner have felt that there should be an immediate start at high intensity. It has been suggested that the best effect can be obtained by alternate seven-day periods at high and low altitudes, and also that there should be an emphasis on speed work in order to increase or

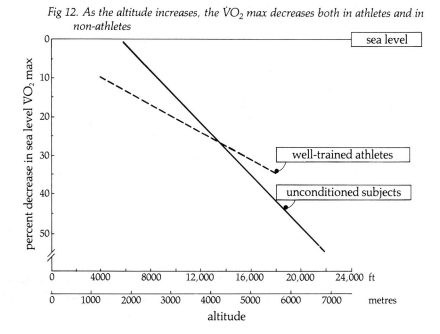

Fig 12. As the altitude increases, the $\dot{V}O_2$ max decreases both in athletes and in non-athletes

maintain muscle power. It should be remembered that *all* recovery is aerobic: for this reason, periods of exertion should be shorter and recovery intervals longer than at sea level.

Some athletes have difficulties with headaches, sleeping badly and gastric disturbances, but these usually disappear within two or three days. The same rules for physiological adaptation to altitude apply as for heat, humidity and time changes (see below), and it is likely that at least eight or ten days' acclimatisation will be needed before the runner is functioning completely normally. People who use pulse rates as a guide to intensity of effort should realise that these are affected by altitude. P. Åstrand and K. Rodahl have recommended increasing your consumption of fluids and carbohydrates.

Favour reported that it took at least three weeks to acclimatise oneself to an altitude of 2,000m (about 6,600ft); but W. H. Weihe believed that two weeks were quite sufficient while Pugh considered that full acclimatisation took months rather than weeks. In view of this conflict among experts, your best plan is probably to follow closely any advice you are given and, above all, to form your own conclusions and act according to what seems best for *you*.

Although this remains a controversial area, it does appear that the benefits of spending time at altitude and training there remain for some ten to

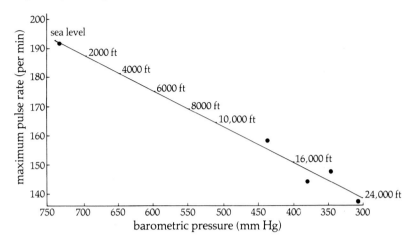

Fig 13. Influence of altitude on the maximum pulse rate

fourteen days after your return to sea level. Many individual athletes and national teams have taken advantage of this fact by training at altitude before major championships.

Travelling

Nowadays many runners combine their holiday with the chance to run a marathon far from home — indeed, there are plenty of package tours available designed exactly for this.

Even if you are travelling only a few hundred kilometres to your race there are some points worth bearing in mind. If you are going by automobile or coach, make sure that your seat is comfortable and that you have adequate ventilation. Try to organise things so that you can stop every two hours or so for a short stroll. Any meals which you eat *en route* should be light — fresh fruit and sandwiches are ideal.

TRAVELLING BY AIR

Travelling to another country can be more complicated, especially if by air.

Modern aircraft fly at very high altitudes and so their interiors must be artificially pressurised — usually to the level found normally between altitudes of 1,500 and 2,100m (5,000 and 7,000ft). This reduction from the sea-level atmospheric pressure you are used to can cause problems.

The expansion of stomach and intestinal gases can result in a feeling of nausea and minor abdominal cramps — some people experience quite violent pains. Your best way of avoiding this difficulty is to forego starchy and easily fermentable foods both before and during the flight. Drink still fruit juices rather than beer or other fizzy drinks.

Pain is sometimes experienced also in the sinuses, especially those in the frontal and maxillary areas (either side of the nose and jaw), as well as in the ears. If there is any mucous congestion — e.g., if you have a cold — this can cause pain in the region of the face and forehead. The only solution to this would appear to be to make sure you don't have a cold when you climb on board an aircraft!

The reduced pressure in the aircraft cabin also lowers the humidity of the atmosphere to a level rarely greater than 25 per cent. This may cause minor dehydration problems, so make sure that you drink enough. Some people have trouble with dry lips and mouths, and contact-lens wearers can have particular trouble with dry eyes. Making sure that you drink enough will help here, too; and, if you wear contact lenses, it is obviously a good idea to remove them, wearing spectacles instead if need be.

Some people have problems with swollen feet. Some airlines provide disposable slippers but many do not, so it is a good idea to pack a pair of your own into your flight-bag so that you can change into them before take-off.

Some people recommend wearing a tracksuit for long flights. Certainly tracksuits are comfortable garments to lounge and even sleep in, so this seems an eminently sensible idea. You may find it worthwhile, if you think you are likely to be troubled by aircraft noise, to take earplugs with you.

Nowadays aircraft routinely fly at speeds of around 800km/h (500mph). If you are travelling more than about 2,500km (1,560 miles) north or south you will almost certainly have to contend with an abrupt climatic change. Here the advice given on preparation for hot and cold conditions (see pages 82−90) should be followed.

BIOLOGICAL CLOCKS

Air travel over any substantial distance in either an east-to-west or a west-to-east direction produces the phenomenon known as jetlag. In order to understand jetlag you have to appreciate that the body has a series of inbuilt rhythms. (These are *not* to be confused with the so-called 'biorhythms', which have a scientific status on a par with that of astrology. Biorhythms, it is claimed, are primarily dependent upon birth-dates, and govern our 'physical', 'creative' and 'sensitive' cycles. Our own interest in biorhythms waned rather abruptly when an athlete we know ran a time of 2 hours and 12 minutes in his debut marathon on a day on which all three of his biorhythm cycles were at rock bottom.)

Biological rhythms generally coincide with overt environmental changes — for example, the 24-hour cycle of night and day. However, even if the environment itself shows a different cycle, the biological rhythm has a tendency to continue much as usual, although with a period slightly different from the normal one (hence the term 'circadian', from the Latin *circa*, 'about', and *dies*, 'day'). The body can be regarded, therefore, as having an internal 'clock' — or, more accurately, a set of clocks.

The major daily cycles in human beings are those relating to rest/activity (i.e., sleeping/waking) patterns; temperature, electrolyte excretion and cortisol production have all been extensively studied in this respect. In normal conditions many external cues — e.g., the light/dark cycle, temperature variation, social-activity patterns and knowledge of clock-time — maintain biological rhythms, but the range of frequency to which these rhythms can be entrained is limited: a five- to six-hour time-difference, such as is encountered on crossing the Atlantic, causes a major disruption. The various rhythms require different lengths of time — from days to weeks — to become reentrained to local time.

The time taken to adjust to westward flight is known to be about 50 per cent shorter than that taken to adjust to eastward flight, but the reasons for this are unclear. Some authors have explained this by pointing out that travelling westwards necessitates merely adjusting to the fact that one has had one day which was rather longer than usual (rather as if you had been up half the night at a party: adjustment can be brought about by sleeping it off the morning after), whereas eastward flight more commonly involves adjusting to a more fundamental disturbance of sleeping patterns involving the permanent loss of one night's sleep. K. E. Klein, H. M. Wegman and others have suggested that you can at least partially insulate yourself from the effects of jetlag by altering your meal-times for a few days before you travel so that they correspond more closely to those of your destination. Dr Michael Selson is another who supports the simple loss-of-sleep theory in explaining the difference in adjustment times between 'eastward' and 'westward' jetlag.

It has been estimated that it takes between three and seven days for the body to adjust to an eight- to ten-hour eastward journey (London to Tokyo, for example). Generally speaking, you are recommended to allow yourself 24 to 48 hours of rest after arrival, and then to spend the next few days easing yourself back into normal training schedules. Your adjustment programme might look like this:

O disembarkation day: *rest*, no training
O day 1: 5km (about 3¼ miles) of easy running, assuming you normally run about 10km (6¼ miles) daily
O day 2: 7.5km (about 4¾ miles) of medium-paced running
O day 3: 10km (6¼ miles) running as usual

Local clock-time changes by one hour for every 15 degrees of longitude traversed, so that (allowing for flight time) an early-morning flight from London will arrive in New York a little after local lunchtime. However, your body feels that it is late afternoon or early evening; and by mid-evening, local time, it will be feeling that it is time to go to bed. You should not succumb to this completely: instead of going to bed four hours early, when you will almost certainly be unable to get to sleep, force yourself to stay up until one and a half to two hours before your normal bedtime. Over the next day or two, adjust this gradually, so that by the third day you are operating at local time.

The situation is easier if you take an evening flight from London to New York. Although your body will feel that it is the early hours of the morning, you are likely to arrive at about what is, according to local clocks, a reasonable bedtime. By simply going to bed and allowing yourself to wake at what is, locally, a reasonable hour of the morning, you can get much the same effect as if you were sleeping off a late night.

In all cases remember that adaptation to most environmental conditions and changes requires a period of between four and eight days. You cannot force nature along: you must make compromises with it.

It is worth looking at the comments of Bill Adcocks, a marathon runner whose heyday was the 1960s. Representing the UK, he was the silver medallist in the 1966 Commonwealth Games, finished sixth in the 1970 Commonwealth Games, and was fifth in the 1968 Olympics in Mexico City; in addition, he chalked up wins in Fukuoka (1968), Karl Marx Stadt and Athens (1969) and Otsu-Maihicki (1970).

For his Fukuoka run, his air-travel time was over 15 hours, and he had to adjust to an 11-hour time-difference ('so internal time clock opposite to normal'). He arrived in Japan six days before the race, which was run on Sunday 8 December. At home he had been running more than 100 miles (160km) per week — two weeks at 116 miles (185.6km) and one at 105 miles (168km) before the race. In Japan he ran only 65 miles (104km) before the race, running not at all on the day of his arrival and refraining from running hard before the Wednesday. After the first two nights he reported that his sleep pattern was 'good'.

Interestingly enough, Bill reports that when he returned to Japan more recently in the new capacity of team manager he took twice as long to adjust to the time-change; this he attributes to the fact that, while he is still trim and moderately fit, he is of course not nearly as fit as he used to be — in other

---

Bill Adcocks ran many under-distance races in his career, particularly on the track

words, he feels that fitness is a definite factor in the time it takes you to adjust. Whether or not this is the case, experts have found that age is certainly a factor.

Adcocks sums up with an excellent piece of advice: 'Try to make everything leading up to a race abroad as normal as it would be if you were at home.'

GENERAL PRECAUTIONS

If you travel abroad to race or train, be sure that your general health is safeguarded. Travel to tropical and subtropical countries entails serious health risks — from, for example, poliomyelitis — and so you should ensure that you are adequately protected by having had all the relevant 'shots'. If you go to an area where malaria is prevalent, be sure to take with you adequate supplies of antimalarial drugs and to use them in the prescribed doses.

Travellers' diarrhoea is a common complaint, typically lasting from one to three days and arriving with alarming suddenness. Often there is no identifiable pathogenic agent, but a few simple rules may help avoid the problem. If you are in any doubt at all about the drinking water, drink only bottled water or soft drinks (and do not then add ice, because the ice will almost certainly be from the local water). Never rewarm cooked food; avoid shellfish and seafood generally; peel all fruit, after washing it thoroughly; and never buy food, including drinks and ice cream, from street vendors.

Above all, as Adcocks says, try to create conditions abroad which are as close as possible to those to which you are accustomed at home.

4 Diet *John Humphreys*

If you are training hard to run the 42km or so of a marathon then any aids which may help your performance should be carefully considered. Obviously, diet alone cannot make you achieve a personal record, but a *suitable* diet will be a contributing factor in the improvement of your performance.

Essential nutrients

The optimum diet for the marathon runner supplies water, protein, fats, carbohydrates, minerals and vitamins in adequate amounts and in the correct proportions. Because of the high energy expenditure in marathon training, you need a greater caloric intake to maintain body weight than does the more sedentary person. It must be realised, however, that *excessive* caloric intake — that is, more than your body actually uses up — may lead to obesity and is therefore not recommended. Specific components of food (nutrients) satisfy three basic body needs: energy; tissue repair and the formation of new tissue; and chemical regulation of metabolic processes.

Of all the substances you ingest, water is probably the most important, since the body requires a constant, uninterrupted supply for the production of energy, temperature control and elimination of waste products. Reduced water supply decreases the endurance (circulo-respiratory) capacity and results in rapid fatigue.

FATS AND CARBOHYDRATES

According to Åstrand, the intensity of work in relation to the athlete's maximum aerobic power affects the proportion of nutritional energy that can be derived from fats and carbohydrates. It is reported that fat supplied 50 – 60 per cent of the energy in subjects engaged in light to moderate continuous exercise, whereas during prolonged continuous work fat represented, in increasing amounts, up to 70 per cent of the energy fuel.

High-carbohydrate diets (in which 70 per cent or so of the Calories in the athlete's diet are from carbohydrate foods) have been shown to increase work performance in heavy, exhausting exercise by giving a better energy-yield per litre of oxygen than either high-fat or high-protein diets. In general, carbohydrates will increase your glycogen stores (see page 108). The higher the glycogen stores, the better your potential marathon performance.

ENERGY SOURCES

The marathon is essentially an aerobic event — in other words, the runner needs to process large amounts of oxygen for sustained periods of time. In marathon running the availability and utilisation of energy sources stored in the body (fat and glycogen) are very important.

During the early stages of a marathon, carbohydrates supply as much as 90 per cent of the energy, with fats providing 10 per cent or less. However, as the race progresses, a larger fraction of the energy is obtained from fats and proportionately less from carbohydrates. In the latter part of the run as much as 95 — 98 per cent of the runner's energy may be derived from free fatty acids.

It should be appreciated that muscle glycogen is an essential fuel for sustained muscular effort. Research has demonstrated that, if a runner starts a marathon race with low muscle and/or liver glycogen concentrations, his glycogen stores will be exhausted early on so that he will be unable to finish the race. Glycogen is used up most rapidly during the early stages of a race, and so the athlete who runs too fast at this point may prematurely deplete his glycogen stores and so affect his performance drastically. It is possible to boost glycogen stores in the muscles by dietary control, as we shall see (page 108).

PROTEINS

The major role of proteins in the body is in the building of new body tissue. A nutritionally adequate diet of normal foods will provide a protein intake sufficient for marathon training and racing. Special pre-race high-protein diets (e.g., steaks) are not required by the marathon runner — in fact, they are counterproductive.

According to the National Research Council of the United States, the daily recommended intake of protein is about 0.9 grams of protein per kilogram of body weight (about 0.2oz per stone).

VITAMINS AND MINERALS

Minerals are divided into two groups — those required by the body in comparatively large amounts, and those it needs in only small quantities (trace minerals). Potassium, phosphorus, calcium, sodium, magnesium and sulphur belong to the first group, while at least fourteen trace minerals need to be ingested to maintain the best of health — of these, iron, iodine and zinc are vital for successful body function.

Vitamins (fat-soluble and water-soluble) are needed in small amounts; they serve as chemical regulators and are crucial to growth and the maintenance of life. The fourteen known vitamins can all be obtained in sufficient quantities from a nutritionally balanced diet. Extra vitamin supplements, such as B-complex vitamin pills, are probably of little value and are unlikely to improve your endurance capacity.

An important change in mineral metabolism that may be caused by marathon training is the loss of salt (sodium chloride). Sweat contains 20−30mmol of sodium per litre. Excessive sweating from strenuous physical exercise can lead to sodium losses of as much as 350mmol/day, or even more. For the non-acclimatised individual, this amount would be enough to disturb the balance of fluids (homeostasis) within the body. The salt intake of marathon runners therefore needs to be greater than the average adult's 6−18g/day, which contains 100 to 300mmol of sodium. Excessive salt intake, however, is to be avoided, since it will increase the quantity of water you require to drink and could result in greater water retention; this, in turn, could affect your efficiency during training. The best plan is to take just a little more salt with your food than usual. You should avoid taking salt tablets, as this practice has been known to result in gastro-intestinal disturbances.

IRON

Iron is an essential mineral for everybody, but especially for endurance athletes: it is well established that there is no chance of your running a marathon at your best if you are anaemic.

Iron combines with protein to make haemoglobin, the red substance in blood that transports oxygen from the lungs to the body cells and removes carbon dioxide from the cells. The average haemoglobin content for men is approximately 14.7g/100ml (0.15oz/fl oz) of blood and for women 13.7g/100ml (0.14oz/fl oz), but values higher than this may be expected in the fully trained marathon runner. Women can lose up to 70ml (about 2.5 fl oz) of blood during the menstrual period, a significant loss of iron; this means that women are more likely to be anaemic and in need of iron therapy.

Runners suffering from iron deficiency may experience a sudden deterioration in training or racing performance, breathlessness, headaches and insomnia. If you have several of these symptoms together you should think about a visit to your doctor for a blood test. The doctor may recommend an injection or therapy using iron preparations together with vitamin C or various iron-based tablets such as ferrous gluconate. Excessive iron supplementation should be avoided, since it can prove toxic to the liver.

Only a few foods contain much iron: liver is a particularly good source, but kidney, heart, lean meats, shellfish, potatoes, dry beans, dry peas, dark green vegetables, dried fruit and egg yolk are all rich in iron. Whole-grain and enriched bread and cereals contain smaller amounts of iron, but when eaten frequently become important sources.

Iron-deficiency anaemia is only one of several types of anaemia. Another can occur should you be suffering from a deficiency of the vitamin folic acid, which is to be found in meat but especially in green vegetables. However, in general there is no real need to worry about anaemia of any sort if you normally eat a good, mixed diet.

Water and drinking

Water is essential for life: people usually die within a week if deprived of it. It is of course fundamental to the mechanism whereby body heat can be dissipated through the evaporation of sweat. Because body-heat production is greatly increased during physical exercise, more water is lost through sweating, and this water must be replaced. Should your body temperature rise and remain for an extended period above normal, you may eventually suffer from heat stroke (see page 89). It is therefore imperative to increase fluid intake as the work level and environmental temperature increase, to maintain fluid balance. Scientific evidence strongly favours the practice of replacing water loss by intermittent fluid intake.

Many electrolyte aids are now on the market — e.g., gatorade, dietaid, accolade, sportade, and bike half-time punch — and, although they vary in their electrolyte concentration, they all contain sodium, potassium and carbohydrates. Arguably water is just as good, or perhaps a lemon-flavoured glucose drink. Guidelines on drinks for marathon runners are given below.

Table 13 *Drinks for marathon runners*

CONTENT OF DRINK

The drink should be:

- O hypotonic — few solid particles per unit of water
- O low in sugar content — less than 2.5g/100ml ($^1/_{40}$oz/fl oz)
- O cold — roughly 8−13 degrees C (46−55 degrees F)
- O palatable — it will be consumed in volumes of 100−400ml ($3^1/_2$−14 fl oz)

AMOUNT TO BE DRUNK BEFORE COMPETITION

400−600ml (14−21 fl oz) of water, or of the above drink, 30 minutes before the start of competition

AMOUNT TO BE DRUNK DURING COMPETITION

100−200ml ($3^1/_2$−7 fl oz) of the above drink should be taken at 10- to 15-minute intervals

POST-COMPETITION DIET

modest salting of foods and ingestion of drinks with essential minerals can
adequately replace the electrolytes (sodium and potassium) lost in sweat

DETECTION OF DEHYDRATION

keep a record of early-morning body weight (after urination, before breakfast)
so that any symptoms of chronic dehydration can soon be detected

VALUE OF DRINKS

significant in races lasting more than 50 or 60 minutes

DRINKING WHILE RUNNING

Marathon feed bottles typically hold about 220ml (7½ fl oz). Several bottles
may be carried in your jogger pouch; it is a good idea to put some padding,
such as a tee-shirt, in the bag to stop the bottles bouncing about.

If you are undertaking long sustained training runs, particularly on hot
days, practise taking several gulps from your bottle periodically, so that you
perfect this skill in advance of your marathon race. You should certainly take
fluid during long runs, especially if they are of more than 50−60 minutes'
duration. Make a point of drinking when you are running slowly: it is much
harder to drink when running at speed.

During a marathon race, the availability of water should be unrestricted.
It is important to remember, however, that large amounts of water (i.e., more
than a few gulps) should not be taken at any one time, as this may lead to a
full, uncomfortable feeling. You need to drink frequently, as and when
required: in a marathon run in the heat this may be as often as every 10−15

Feed bottles

A typical jogger pouch

minutes. Drinking fluids will reduce your degree of dehydration and consequently lower the stress load placed on the circulatory system.

When swallowing you cannot breathe; therefore it is suggested you take several small gulps from feed bottles. However, in large-field marathons there are no personal prepared drinks, only cups with drinks supplied by the organisers. The average runner, particularly on a hot or humid day, should stop for a few seconds to drink properly from these cups. If you try to drink when running quickly, it will make you prone to sickness and stitches.

You may seriously damage your health if you do not drink during the race — for example, you may suffer heat stroke (see page 89) — so make sure that you get the liquid you need. There have been several cases of athletes dying during marathons run on hot days through failure to drink enough.

Fig 14. Procedure at feeding station

Direction of running

→

personal drinks   water and squash   sponges

When you arrive at a feeding station you will find the drinks laid out on tables (on your right in most countries, but on your left in the UK). First will be the table bearing the personal drinks of the athletes (not applicable in large-field marathons); then the tables with cups of water and/or squash; and finally a table for damp sponges. Your procedure at the feeding station should be as follows:

○ take your personal drink and transfer it to your other hand, holding your thumb over the top of the bottle (not applicable during mass marathons when only cups are available)
○ take a cup of water and pour it over your head
○ sponge the large muscle groups, particularly your thighs; include your neck and wrists
○ drink slowly, allowing for recovery of breathing between gulps; use any unfinished drink to cool yourself by, for example, pouring it over your head

Always start a run well hydrated (see Table 13, page 104), and remember that it is much easier to drink early in the race, when you are still fresh, than it is in the latter stages. The first feeding station usually occurs at the 5km (3-mile) mark, and other feeding stations occur at regular intervals thereafter.

Drinking after a race run in the heat will result in a significant loss of electrolytes. Excessive electrolyte losses are adequately met by adding a little more salt to your food.

250ml (8¾ fl oz) of orange juice will replace most of the potassium and most, if not all, of the calcium and magnesium lost in 2−3 litres (3½−5¼ Imperial pints, 4¼−6⅓ US pints) of sweat. Tomato juice is equally effective in supplementing the dietary intake of most essential minerals.

Classification of foods

Before we move on to pre- and post-marathon meals it should be appreciated that fats and carbohydrates are fuel nutrients; that protein, trace mineral elements and water are necessary for the building of tissue; and that mineral salts and vitamins act as body regulators. There are in fact a total of 35−40 different nutrients essential for normal nutrition.

Foods can be classified into four basic groups, according to their respective roles in the diet, as shown in Table 14. Your normal nutritional diet should include foods from each of the four groups, but the relative amounts you eat will vary depending upon which diet-loading method you use (see pages 108−121).

Table 14 *Classification of foods*

GRAIN PRODUCTS

bread, flour, cereals, baked foods (whole-grain or enriched preferred)
role in diet: to provide protein, carbohydrates, minerals, and B vitamins (high-energy-yielding foods)
amount: four or more servings per day

MEAT AND RELATED FOODS

red meats, poultry, fish, shellfish (dried beans, peas and nuts are alternatives)
role in diet: to provide protein, fats, iron and certain other minerals, and B vitamins
amount: servings every meal (except red meats)

DAIRY PRODUCTS

milk, cheese, ice cream, eggs, butter, margarine
role in diet: to provide protein, fats, calcium, and other minerals and vitamins
amount: four or more daily servings

VEGETABLES AND FRUIT

role in diet: to provide minerals, vitamin C and other vitamins, dietary fibre, folic acid, and iron
amount: four or more daily servings

A carbohydrate-loading diet

Since the classic studies of Christensen and Hansen (1939), it has been established that dietary manipulation can significantly increase the glycogen content of the muscles. J. Bergström *et al.* (1966) observed that, after a normal mixed diet giving an initial glycogen content of 1.75g/100g wet muscle (0.28oz/lb), a subject could tolerate a work-load demanding an average of 75 per cent of his or her maximum oxygen uptake for about 115 minutes. After the subject had spent three days on an extreme fat and protein diet, the glycogen concentration was reduced to about 0.6g/100g wet muscle (0.01oz/lb), and the standard load could be undertaken for only about 60 minutes. Following three days on a carbohydrate-rich diet, the subject's glycogen content rose to 3.5g/100g wet muscle (0.56oz/lb), and the 75 per cent load could now be sustained for 170 minutes (all figures averages).

Fig 15. Percentage of carbohydrates in commonly served foods

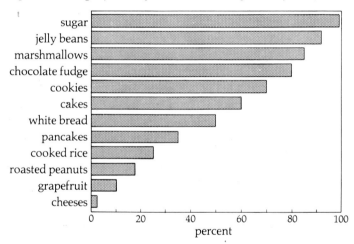

The carbohydrate-rich diet was more effective if the muscles were initially depleted of glycogen through prolonged strenuous exercise, in the form of a 15km (9⅜-mile) fast continuous run. The low level could then be maintained by use of a low-carbohydrate diet for a few days. If this were followed by a few days on a high-carbohydrate diet, the glycogen content of the muscles could be made to exceed 4g/100g (0.64oz/lb), and the 75 per cent load could be tolerated for over four hours; in other words, the body's total glycogen content could be built up to more than 700g (1lb 9oz). Since the higher the initial glycogen content of the muscles before a race, the better your performance is likely to be, it is worth looking in some detail at carbohydrate-loading diets. (We shall return to other glycogen-loading techniques later — see page 116.)

Fig 16. *Effects of a mixed diet, a low-carbohydrate diet, and a high-carbohydrate diet on the glycogen content of the quadriceps femoris and the duration of exercise on a bicycle ergometer. These data clearly show that the higher the initial level of muscle glycogen, the greater the endurance for submaximal exercise*

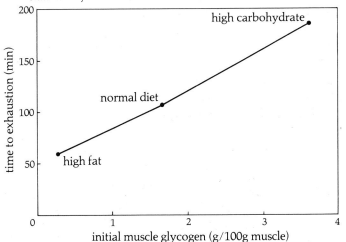

Fig 17. *Effects of muscle glycogen on competitive endurance performance. The fall-off in the runner's pace is attributable to a drop in the muscle glycogen level to less than 3g/kg ($^1/_{20}$ oz/lb). If the athlete is to maintain an optimal pace during competitive endurance performance, muscle glycogen levels must be sufficiently elevated (e.g., by diet) to provide more than 3g/kg concentration from start to finish*

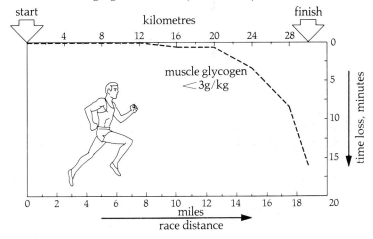

A successful and tolerable carbohydrate-loading regime requires a reasonably balanced and adequate diet over the six or seven days for which the regime will last. For you to select a balanced diet you have to understand the basic principles involved in the calculation of your carbohydrate intake.

Virtually all common foods consist of a mixture of carbohydrate, fat and protein in varying proportions (a notable exception is sugar, which is pure carbohydrate). The normal energy intake of an adult human being — i.e., the number of Calories in his or her food — is typically divided up as follows: 10 per cent from protein, 40 per cent from fat and 50 per cent from carbohydrate. Translating this into the actual weights of foods consumed, we find that each gram of protein contains 4 Calories, each gram of carbohydrate 4 Calories, and each gram of fat 9 Calories (protein 113Cal/oz, carbohydrate 113Cal/oz, fat 255Cal/oz). So, if you know the weights of protein, fat and carbohydrate that you typically eat (by weighing your food and looking up the relevant values in published tables), you can calculate, in Calories, your actual energy intake.

Conversely, and rather less precisely, you can derive from published tables an estimate of the number of Calories you consume each day and, depending upon your weight, sex, lifestyle, etc., calculate how much protein, fat and carbohydrate you are eating. For example, if on average you consume 4,000Cal per day, about half of this — i.e., 2,000Cal — you will normally be ingesting in the form of carbohydrates. Since you know that each gram of carbohydrate produces 4Cal, you can easily calculate that you are eating about 500g (17²⁄₃oz) of carbohydrate daily.

In order to design a well balanced, nutritionally sound diet suited to your personal tastes and requirements you should, therefore, adopt the following procedure.

O   Estimate your normal carbohydrate intake in grams, either by assuming a typical value for your total daily energy intake, as in the example above, or, preferably, by consulting Tables 15 to 17 (see pages 112−113). You will need to write down a typical day's consumption of food — ideally, you should measure out the portions — and then compare your meals with the quantities listed in the tables. Note that the sizes of the portions given in the tables do not necessarily correspond to average servings; for example, if you eat four thick slices of toast for breakfast this counts as 8 portions — that is, 80g (2.9oz) of carbohydrate. *Your daily carbohydrate intake should not be less than 280g (10oz)*; if you find that it is, check to make sure that you haven't made a mistake in your calculation and then, if necessary, add extra carbohydrate to your diet.

O   Your carbohydrate intake during the six- or seven-day regime should be as follows: for the first three days, one quarter of the normal value but certainly not less than 70g (2½oz); for the final three or four days, one and a half times the normal value — more if you can manage it.

PLANNING YOUR MEALS

There are two phases involved in the six- or seven-day carbohydrate-loading regime, the initial low-carbohydrate phase and the succeeding high-carbohydrate phase.

The low-carbohydrate phase: If you have been put on a low-fat diet for medical reasons you should consult your doctor before embarking on this phase. If at any time during it you feel nauseous or get a headache, take two teaspoonsful of sugar in a hot drink. Should the symptoms persist, then you would be well advised to consider abandoning the diet.

During this phase you may eat as much as you like of the foods listed in Table 16 (see page 113) except those under the heading 'very little carbohydrate, protein and fat'; of these latter you may eat small quantities, since they contain very limited amounts of carbohydrate. From section C of Table 15 you should select foods in sufficient quantities to make up your allowance of one quarter of your normal carbohydrate intake: the other foods listed in Table 15 should at this stage be avoided, since they are considerably poorer in protein and fat.

Omit from your diet all sugar and sugar-containing foods, and remember to read carefully the labels of packaged foods: many highly unlikely looking savouries contain large quantities of sugar.

The high-carbohydrate phase: Do not follow this part of the diet for more than three or four consecutive days; if you feel unwell, develop chest pains, or whatever, then stop at once. If you are on a prescribed diet — for diabetes, perhaps — you must consult your doctor or dietician before embarking on this phase.

Select foods from sections A and B of Table 15 to make up your allowance of one and a half times your normal carbohydrate intake. In addition, you can eat small quantities of the foods listed in Table 16 under the heading 'very low carbohydrate, very high protein' and as much as you like of those described as 'very little carbohydrate, protein and fat' and 'carbohydrate-"free"'.

Do not use fat in cooking, and eat only 15g (½oz) butter or margarine or 30g (1oz) of a low-fat spread each day. You can drink 150ml (5 fl oz) of milk per day, and as much as you want to of sweetened clear drinks. If you feel hungry, eat more foods from section A of Table 15.

Table 15 *Portions of food containing 10g (⅓oz) of carbohydrate*

tbs = tablespoonful
tsp = teaspoonful

SECTION A

cereals and grain:

1 tbs cooked macaroni
2 tbs oatmeal cooked in water
2 tbs cooked rice
3 tbs unsweetened breakfast cereal

fruit and vegetables:

1 'egg-sized' boiled potato
   or boiled sweet potato
1 boiled medium parsnip
1 medium apple/pear/orange
1 small banana/bunch grapes
2 level tbs sweetened apple sauce
2 tbs fruit (cooked or canned with sugar)
½ cup sweetened fruit juices
¼ cup grape juice
4 dried apricot halves
2 tsp dried raisins or currants
2 dried whole dates

sugar and sugar products:

2 tsp brown or white sugar
2 tsp honey
2 tsp syrup
2 tsp jam or jelly preserve
1 medium meringue
15g (½oz) candy/sweets (not chocolate)

beverages:

½ glass carbonated drink (e.g., cola)
2 tbs Lucozade
300ml (10 fl oz) beer
300ml (10 fl oz) medium cider
1 glass sweet wine
1 wine-glass port

miscellaneous:

1 tbs chutney
2−3 tbs jelly or jello

SECTION B

cereals and grain:

½ thick slice of white or brown bread
1 thin slice of white or brown bread
1 slice of rye or raisin bread
1 large or 2 small biscuits/cookies
   (not chocolate)
1 pancake of 10cm (4in) diameter

vegetables:

1 heaped tbs baked beans or other
   pre-cooked beans (not green) or
   peas
3 tbs fresh or frozen green peas
2 tbs boiled corn

milk:

2 tbs sweetened condensed milk

miscellaneous:

½ cup thickened soup

SECTION C

cereals and grain:

½ doughnut
small piece of cheesecake

milk and dairy:

1 glass of milk
4 tbs natural yogurt
2 tbs sweetened flavoured yogurt
1 scoop ice cream

vegetables:

12 french fries or 6 chips

meat and fish:

2 fish fingers (breaded)

sugar and confectionery:

30g (1oz) chocolate

Table 16 *Foods containing low amounts of carbohydrate*

very low carbohydrate, very high protein:*

egg	cured meats
fresh meat, including minced beef (hamburger)	all-meat sausages
	hard cheese
fowl	single cream
fresh or frozen fish (not in sauce or batter)	nuts (maximum 4 tbs)
	peanut butter

trace amounts of carbohydrate, very high fat:

oil	butter/margarine
lard	double cream

very little carbohydrate, protein and fat:*

green beans	tomatoes, radish, celery, raw carrots, cabbage
all green leaf vegetables	mushrooms, onions
courgettes/zucchini, green peppers, cucumber	grapefruit, rhubarb (sweetened with non-sugar sweetener)

carbohydrate-'free':

marmite/bovril/bouillon	coffee/tea/mineral waters/'low-calorie' carbonated beverages
salt/mustard/pepper	

---

* When following a low-carbohydrate diet these foods may be cooked in fat — i.e., fried — but on a high-carbohydrate diet they must be cooked and eaten without fat

Table 17 *Foods containing high amounts of carbohydrate in an average portion*

	carbohydrate content	
	g	oz
1 slice sponge cake (no topping)	30	1
1 small portion of fruit cake, plain	20	⅔
1 portion of fruit pie or crumble	50	1¾
1 plain cup/fairy cake	25	⅞
1 small '6 inch diameter' pizza	50	1¾

Foods to be avoided

Foods to be generally avoided during training, and particularly in the period leading up to a marathon race, include

○ underdone starchy foods; e.g., hot cakes, muffins, etc.
○ highly spiced or peppery foods
○ gas-forming foods; e.g., cabbage, onions and beans
○ any greasy or fried foods that are hard to digest; e.g., fried pork chops
○ laxatives and mineral oils
○ antacids

Do not over-eat before running — the stomach should be relatively empty. Chew your food well to break it down into a semi-liquid state. Do not eat any foods that you know will disagree with you, especially those which might give you indigestion.

Pre-run meal

The pre-run meal should be taken three hours before the race and should include only small amounts of fat and protein since these are slow to digest and do not provide fuels that can be readily utilised during the early stages of the event. A light carbohydrate meal is recommended — something like cereal, oatmeal or toast with honey. Also, you should take small amounts of food containing vitamin C. A meal like this should be ideal if taken three hours before the race, although some runners prefer to take it four hours before.

Table 18 *Guidelines to follow in planning the pre-run diet*

ENERGETICS

Energy intake should be adequate to ward off any feelings of hunger or weakness during the entire period of the competition. Although pre-contest food intakes make only a minor contribution to the immediate energy expenditure, they are essential for the support of an adequate level of blood sugar, and for avoiding the sensations of hunger and weakness.

TIMING

The diet plan should ensure that the stomach and upper bowel are empty at the time of competition.

FLUID CONTENT

Food and fluid intakes prior to and during prolonged competition should guarantee an optimal state of hydration.

BLANDNESS

The pre-competition diet should offer foods that will minimise upset in the gastro-intestinal tract.

PSYCHOLOGICAL ASPECTS

The diet should include food with which the athlete is familiar, and which he is convinced will 'make him win'.

No food (except clear drinks) should be ingested during the final 1½ – 2 hours before the competition; this is to prevent temporary elevation of the blood's glucose and insulin levels. Remember not to eat too much for your last meal before the race. Try to find a palatable food that is easy to digest and high in carbohydrate content.

Take only extremely light exercise, if at all, in the 48 hours prior to the race; this is so that your glycogen stores (from carbohydrate foods) in your liver and muscles can be fully built up (see page 102). Experiment with various carbohydrate meals before you go on long runs — i.e., over 25km (15½ miles) — and decide which carbohydrate foods best suit you; it will be too late to decide on the day of the race.

LIQUID MEALS

In many countries nowadays, particularly in the USA, liquid meals such as Ensure, Ensure Plus, Nutriment, Sustagen and Sustan Cal are used. Many of these are excellent, especially for the pre-race meal, because they

O   prevent nausea and dryness of the mouth before the race
O   are absorbed into the system more readily than some solid meals (i.e., they are digested rapidly and completely)
O   provide a rapid source of energy that will improve your endurance capacity during the run
O   are high in carbohydrates yet still contain enough fat and protein to give you a feeling of satiety
O   are in liquid form and so contribute to your fluid needs

Liquid meals may also be of benefit in supplementing your daily Calorie intake if you have difficulty maintaining your body weight, or if you want to increase your body weight. If you decide to take a pre-run liquid meal, you should make sure *before* the competition that you are familiar with its effects on you.

COFFEE

Recently it has been shown that caffeine improves circulo-respiratory endurance capacity. A cup of coffee contains 100—150mg of caffeine, the energy-producing effects of which are probably related to its role in aiding the mobilisation of free fatty acids — the form in which fat is usable as a fuel for the aerobic system. Since caffeine enables more fat to be used as a fuel, less glycogen need be used (see page 102). Glycogen-sparing reduces muscular fatigue — hence the beneficial effect.

Take a cup of coffee one hour before you undertake a long continuous run, and see if it makes any difference to your feelings of fatigue, particularly in the latter stages of the run. Some research has indicated that caffeine ingestion (4—5mg/kg body weight) produces a lessening of the subjective ratings of effort. Do not, however, take coffee on a regular basis as part of your diet.

Glycogen loading

As we have already seen (see page 108), the amount of glycogen available in skeletal muscle can be increased by dietary means to values much higher than normal; and we have looked at the basic principles underlying the design of a high-carbohydrate diet. In the next few pages we shall see how these principles can be put into practice.

Three methods of glycogen loading using a combination of diet and exercise are of interest.

METHOD 1

Following several days on a normal mixed diet — containing approximately 50 per cent carbohydrates, 40 per cent fat and 10 per cent protein, change to a high-carbohydrate diet for three or four days. This will increase your glycogen stores from about 1.5g to approximately 2.5g per 100g of wet muscle (0.24 to 0.4oz/lb). During the period of the high-carbohydrate diet, no exhausting exercise should be undertaken; instead, do short, slow continuous runs. No glycogen-depletion run is required (see page 108). During the high-carbohydrate phase, you should include in your diet small amounts of protein and fat as well. *This method should be adopted for your first few marathon runs.*

Table 19 *Examples of diets suitable for muscle-glycogen loading*

food groups	LOW-CARBOHYDRATE DIET	HIGH-CARBOHYDRATE DIET
	daily amounts	
meats	550—700g (20—25oz)	225g (8oz)
breads & cereals	4 servings	10—16 servings
vegetables	3—4 servings	3—4 servings
fruits	4 servings	10 servings
fats	225—250g (8—9oz)	110—170g (4—6oz)
desserts	1—2 servings (only fruits and unsweetened jellies)	2 servings (include ice cream, biscuits, etc.)
beverages	unlimited (no sugar)	unlimited (assuming proper Calorie control)

meals	sample meal plans	
breakfast	225g (8oz) unsweetened orange juice 4 eggs 1 slice toast 4 tsp butter or margarine 4 strips bacon	225g (8oz) orange juice (may be sweetened) 1 egg 2 slices toast 2 tsp butter or margarine 1 cup cereal
lunch	1 meat sandwich (with butter or margarine and mayonnaise) 2—3 cheese sticks 1 tossed salad with oil 1 medium apple or orange	2 sandwiches, each with 30g (1oz) meat or cheese, ½ tsp butter or margarine 225g (8oz) low-fat milk 2 large bananas
dinner	280g (10oz) meat (not ham) 1 small baked potato with 1 tsp butter or margarine and 1 tbs sour cream 1 serving of vegetables (not corn), with 1—2 tsp butter or margarine 1 tossed salad 1 small apple 1 commercial 'diet' dessert	110g (4oz) meat (not ham) 1 medium baked potato with 1 tsp butter or margarine and 1 tbs sour cream 1 serving of vegetables 2 rolls, with 1 tsp butter or margarine 2 servings fruit 2 servings commercial 'diet' beverage
snacks	2 meat sandwiches (with butter or margarine) 1 cheese stick 1 medium apple or banana	2 sandwiches 1 serving of fruit 225g (8oz) low-fat milk

METHOD 2

Here the glycogen-depletion run is undertaken four days before the race: assuming you are a fully trained runner, you should undertake something like a 15km (9½-mile) fast continuous run on the Tuesday prior to a Saturday race. Only limited carbohydrates should be eaten during the rest of Tuesday; but then a high-carbohydrate diet with small amounts of protein and fat should be eaten on Wednesday, Thursday and Friday. This three-day diet raises the glycogen concentration to a level 2½−3 times normal resting levels, as opposed to the seven-day diet's increase of 3−3½ times normal resting levels. This procedure may well result in very little by way of pronounced oxidative muscle changes (detraining effects compared with the seven-day diet). Once again, only light exercise should be undertaken during the three days of the carbohydrate diet. On the three-day diet it is also possible, before the Tuesday depletion run, to eat mostly protein and fat with only a small amount of carbohydrates on the Monday.

Provided you are fully trained and have been in regular training for at least a year, the three-day diet may be used if you intend to compete in several marathons and half-marathons in a single year. It may also be used for 10-mile (16km) road races, particularly if the race is over hilly ground. With the three-day diet you obviously have to be fit enough to recover from a hard, fast continuous run on the Tuesday to race on the Saturday. Table 20 shows an example of a three-day diet that was successfully used prior to the K & M 15-mile (24km) road race in 1978. The runner in question had a best 10-mile road time of 47 minutes and 48 seconds.

Note that the glycogen depletion run was on Tuesday, and that the speed run would be considerably slower than this for the average runner. For the normal athlete one fast (though not flat-out), continuous depletion run — perhaps 10 miles (16km) — on Tuesday is recommended.

The training load for the three-day diet week will depend partly on the runner's previous training state, but it is important that only light exercise is undertaken on the carbohydrate-diet days.

Table 20 *Specimen diet and exercise scheme for a 15-mile (24km) road race*

	morning	afternoon/evening
Sunday	18-mile (28.8km) continuous run at average 6min/mile (3¾min/km)	
Monday	8-mile (12.8km) continuous run at average 6min/mile (3¾min/km)	10-mile (16km) continuous run at average 6min/mile (3¾min/km)
Tuesday	6-mile (9.6km) continuous run at average 6min/mile (3¾min/km)	fast 6-mile (9.6km) continuous run at under 6min/mile (3¾min/km); *plus* 4 × 800m flat out with 2min recovery periods
Wednesday		8- to 10-mile (12.8−16km) continuous run at average 7min/mile (4⅜min/km) *mostly carbohydrate*
Thursday		6-mile (9.6km) continuous run at average 7min/mile (4⅜min/km) *mostly carbohydrate meal with small amounts of protein and fat*
Friday		4-mile (6.4km) continuous run at average 7min/mile (4⅜min/km) *mostly carbohydrate meal with small amounts of protein and fat*
Saturday	*carbohydrate meal 3 hours before race*	K & M 15-mile (24km) road race
Sunday		10-mile (16km) continuous run at average 7min/mile (4⅜min/km)

METHOD 3

In the past this has probably been the most common pre-marathon dietary regime. Here the procedure of glycogen loading covers a seven-day cycle (Saturday to the Friday preceding a Saturday race). A week before the race a fast, continuous long run should be undertaken — say 15−20km (9½−12½ miles) — and this may then be followed by some interval running. This will exhaust the muscles and deplete the glycogen stores. Although the depletion run should be hard, which is necessary if a subsequent boost in the glycogen stores is to occur, it must not be at maximum effort as, in some athletes, this could lead to a physiological peaking at the wrong time. Carbohydrates should not be eaten to excess following this depletion run: take only small amounts for the next three days (Sunday, Monday and Tuesday) and concentrate mainly on proteins and fats. This will maintain low levels of muscle glycogen. Following the three days of primarily protein and fat intake, allow three days (Wednesday, Thursday and Friday) for a mainly carbohydrate diet — although small amounts of fat and protein should still be eaten. During both the protein-and-fat days and the carbohydrate days of the diet, take only light continuous exercise. In the wake of this regime, the glycogen stores in your muscles can exceed 40g/kg (0.64oz/lb). This may result in as much as 700g (1lb 9oz) of stored glycogen, equivalent to 2,800Cal of ready energy. A normal amount for all the muscles of the body would be 400g (14¼oz) of glycogen.

A modification of this method is to do your depletion run instead on the Sunday before a Saturday race. In this case, you switch from a diet consisting mainly of protein and fat to a high-carbohydrate diet after Wednesday lunchtime.

An example of the seven-day diet is shown in Table 21. The light continuous running can be undertaken morning, afternoon or evening, but early evening is recommended if possible. Many people find running more difficult in the early morning than in the late evening, probably because of a slowing-down of their biological clocks overnight.

You should use the seven-day diet only twice a year at most. *Once you are fully trained* you may try the three-day diet to see which of the two works best for you.

Table 21 *Specimen seven-day glycogen-loading diet*

	morning	afternoon/evening
Saturday		depletion run — i.e., fast continuous 12 miles (19.2km) *no carbohydrates eaten following run on Saturday*
Sunday	light 10 miles (16km) continuous	*mostly protein and fat, small amounts of carbohydrate*
Monday	light 10 miles (16km) continuous	*mostly protein and fat, small amounts of carbohydrate*
Tuesday	light 8 miles (12.8km) continuous	*mostly protein and fat, small amounts of carbohydrate*
Wednesday	light 6 miles (9.6km) continuous	*mostly carbohydrate, small amounts of fat and protein*
Thursday	light 4 miles (6.4km) continuous	*mostly carbohydrate, small amounts of fat and protein*
Friday	light 2 miles (3.2km) or rest	*mostly carbohydrate, small amounts of fat and protein*
Saturday	*light carbohydrate meal at 12 noon*	RACE 3pm
Sunday	light easy 6-mile (9.6km) continuous run	

MUSCLE GLYCOGEN-LOADING SIDE-EFFECTS

The daily caloric intake should be normal during all phases of the three diets discussed. A higher than normal caloric intake is undesirable because it may result in weight gain, elevated blood-fat levels and indigestion.

If you are aware that your blood lipid levels are high, avoid any form of glycogen loading as this can affect your metabolism and further increase the lipid levels: for optimum health, this is not a good thing.

Glycogen loading results in an increase in body weight, because each gram of glycogen is stored together with approximately 2.7g of water. If a total glycogen storage of 700g (1lb 9oz) is attained, an increase in body water of 2kg (4lb 3½oz) will result. This means that, if you want to improve upon your best performance, you must examine the type of marathon course and environmental conditions which you will encounter. Where do the hills occur and how many are there? How much weight will you lose, and at what stage of the run? These are all important considerations. In many instances, the weight loss will be greater during a marathon run on a particularly hot or humid day. Note that an increase in water content of a muscle may lead to a feeling of stiffness and heaviness: this may affect your confidence if you are not expecting the response. You need to remember, too, that with glycogen dietary manipulation you may experience feelings of irritability, lethargy and sluggishness. On the positive side, though, the water liberated during glycogen breakdown is made available for temperature regulation when running in the heat.

There have been some cases of myoglobinuria (myoglobin in the urine, which can sometimes result in kidney failure), chest pains and electrocardiogram abnormalities among athletes who regularly use glycogen loading.

Medical opinion has it that rarely, if ever, should such dietary preparations be used for the early adolescent or pre-adolescent runner.

A glycogen-depleted state (i.e., on the protein and fat days) produces a generally weakened condition which may make you more susceptible to infection and injury, and will definitely reduce your capacity to undergo hard training. Although the precise mechanism is not fully understood, glycogen depletion causes an increased level of the glycogen-storing enzyme glycogen-synthetase in the muscle cells. A carbohydrate-rich diet without prior glycogen depletion increases glycogen storage but does not have a boosting or supercompensation effect.

You should carefully record your training response to whichever diet you select to use. This is important because each individual varies in his or her response to specific glycogen diets. D. L. Costill has suggested that one of the most practical ways to monitor muscle glycogen storage is to record your early morning weight after urination and before breakfast: the more you weigh, the more glycogen is stored in your muscles.

Meals following the marathon run

Following a marathon, fats, proteins, carbohydrates, vitamins, minerals and water all need to be replaced. You should wait at least one hour before eating a large meal; but a liquid nutrient may be consumed five to ten minutes after the race in order to stabilise your blood glucose level.

You must select easily digestible foods: these may include cream and butter for fat content, and fish, soft-boiled eggs, cheese and other milk products for protein. Carbohydrates in the form of bread, puddings and rice can be eaten to replace liver and muscle glycogen. Fresh fruit and juices, which are excellent for the replacement of vitamin C, energy and liquid, should always be taken.

Finally, remember to do only light recovery exercise for at least a week, and preferably longer, after the race.

5 Sports injuries and the marathon runner
Ian Adams

Most marathon runners have injury problems, but from a medical point of view these are unspectacular and of a limited variety. They can usually be cured by simply stopping running, and are generally the result of minor abnormalities which are of no significance in the general population; so do not be surprised if your doctor makes little fuss over you but merely advises rest. Some running injuries can be directly treated, some can be indirectly treated, and some simply cannot be treated in the context of the marathoner's regime of running 150km (94 miles) or so per week.

It is a cliché that athletic excellence is brought about by a combination of heredity, training and environment, and these same factors are the ones which, together, govern the extent and nature of sporting injuries.

Heredity controls our shape and our physiology. Just as most of us, however hard we trained, could never become top-class sprinters, so there are others whose bodies are simply not designed to withstand running 150km per week, month after month. The heavier runner, even if carrying no excess fat, gets more injuries than the lighter runner, and also sweats more, so that on long runs fluid replacement is a greater problem.

We may have been born with bow legs or legs of unequal length: these conditions, both of which produce various problems, cannot be treated, but we may be able to do something to reduce their effects — by, for example, building up one shoe. Other biomechanical considerations include the angle of the bone at the hip joint and twisting of the lower leg bones. Many such abnormalities, while untreatable, are very minor deviations from the norm and become of significance only when you are regularly running long distances.

Training is the most important factor in both athletic excellence and the likelihood, or otherwise, of injury. It has to be considered not only from the viewpoint of quantity and quality but also in terms of the environment in which it is done — see below. The present concentration on long runs seems to pay off in terms of improved performances but, the longer the distance, the fewer the number of runners who are actually capable of running it. Ignoring the obvious problems such as self-discipline, we all have different breaking points: for one runner, the breaking point might be 120km (75 miles) per week, for another 150km (94 miles), and for another 250km (156 miles).

Fig 18. Characteristics of a good running shoe

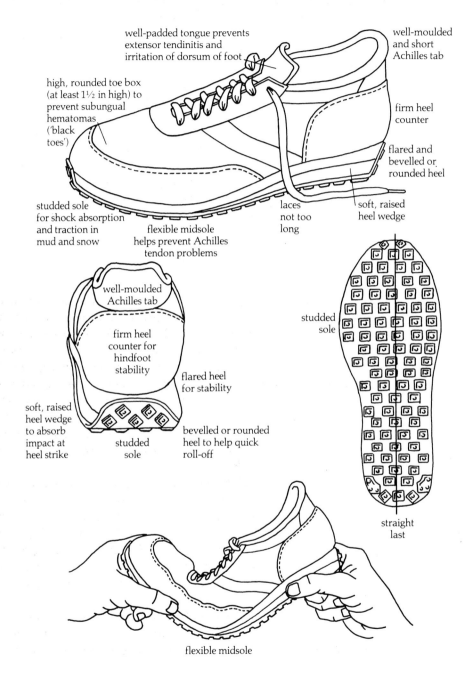

well-padded tongue prevents extensor tendinitis and irritation of dorsum of foot

well-moulded and short Achilles tab

high, rounded toe box (at least 1½ in high) to prevent subungual hematomas ('black toes')

firm heel counter

flared and bevelled or rounded heel

studded sole for shock absorption and traction in mud and snow

flexible midsole helps prevent Achilles tendon problems

laces not too long

soft, raised heel wedge

well-moulded Achilles tab

firm heel counter for hindfoot stability

flared heel for stability

studded sole

soft, raised heel wedge to absorb impact at heel strike

studded sole

bevelled or rounded heel to help quick roll-off

straight last

flexible midsole

Most marathoners have to run long distances on unyielding road surfaces, and this causes abnormally high stresses on the heels and knees: your shoes should therefore be designed as good shock absorbers. Moreover, your running action on the road is different from that on grass or on a Tartan training surface and so, if you have been training for several months on a particular surface, you should allow time for a gradual adjustment to a different one in order to avoid injuries brought about through the abrupt, enforced change of action. The adjustment should be spread over several weeks, during which you spend gradually more time on the different surface.

Emerson said that 'there is a crack in everything God made'; when you run over 150km per week you will discover where the crack in yourself is. A small abnormality in your leg structure (heredity) plus running 150km per week (training) plus doing so on hard surfaces (environment) will sooner or later result in injury. It is therefore well worth your while to attempt to correct or compensate for your physical fault, adjust your training routine, or select a different running surface.

Exercises

The regular running of long distances means that you have little time to do anything else. It means also that the primary muscle groups become well developed and tight in comparison with those muscles which are little used and so grow weak and overstretched. This leads to a muscular imbalance which can cause injuries; flexibility exercises such as those on pages 74—75 therefore become important, especially if you are training over long distances. They are important, too, for the avoidance of hamstring tightness (often associated with pain in the lower back) and tightness of the calf muscles and Achilles tendon (associated with shin splints and flat feet). These exercises take up only about four or five minutes each day, and time simply must be found for them.

The balance of strength between the two legs is important. A minor sprained ankle followed by a premature return to training, with the muscles of the injured leg still below par so that most of the drive comes from the uninjured leg, leading to loss of running style, particularly on hills . . . the injured leg will not regain its strength through the exercise of running, and the whole catalogue comprises a perfect recipe for further injury. You should, therefore, undertake special strengthening exercises, such as step-ups onto a stool (see page 79).

The abdominal muscles are often forgotten by runners. Weakness of the abdominal group allows the pelvis to tilt unnaturally, so that undue stress is placed upon the back: the results are pain and a shortening of the stride-length. There are numerous types of abdominal exercises which can be done to strengthen these muscles (see, for example, pages 76 – 79).

Running style

The style of running varies from one person to the next. Certain aspects of it are as characteristic and unchangeable as our fingerprints, but others can be modified. Try to avoid taking too long a stride: this will cause shin splints and hamstring problems.

Running with the foot turned outwards places twisting strains on the knee, particularly on the kneecap, leading to undue wear on the contact surfaces — this is the painful condition known as 'runner's knee'. You should, therefore, slowly and very consciously 'train' your feet to land correctly. Extreme outward-turning of the feet is often found in association with swinging of one or both arms too far across the body. Correcting the arm action will often solve the foot problem.

Running surfaces

The most important item of your running gear is your shoes: we have already mentioned the need for adequate padding in the heel and forefoot when running on hard surfaces. There has to be a compromise between padding and flexibility: if the padding is too thick the shoe will be inflexible, and this may lead to shin and calf problems. In this as in other matters to do with footwear, the young runner will probably be able to get away with wearing almost anything on his or her feet, but the older runner will have to be much more careful.

Nowadays most shoes for everyday or training use have built-up heels. If you suddenly switch to racing flats, which have a very low heel, and start running, the Achilles tendon and the calf muscles have to adapt to an unaccustomed extra stretch. To avoid injury, flexibility exercises are essential.

The choice between rounded and sharp heels is a matter of personal preference; but my own feeling is that a rounded heel must have a theoretical advantage, since the shape of it spreads the load of the impact as the foot hits the ground. On the subject of heels, heel wear is important. Should the heel be allowed to become too worn down — which usually happens along the outer edge — then the action of the foot in running will alter, thereby causing stress. Heels should, therefore, be mended or replaced regularly — once a month, perhaps.

We have already noted the problems of running on different surfaces, especially hard roads. There are other difficulties. Most pavements are cambered towards the road, so that if you always run on one side of the road you can cause yourself damage: in effect, you are constantly running with one leg slightly shorter than the other.

Running on extremely soft surfaces — e.g., sand — can be pleasant. However, your heels will sink into the surface, and so your Achilles tendon must be flexible if you are to avoid straining it. However, for exactly the same reason, if carefully undertaken then running in sand can be a good stretching exercise.

In much the same way, running uphill stretches the tendon — particularly if you go in for the Lydiard type of bounding. Go carefully if there is any suggestion of Achilles tightness or shin splints.

More of a problem is downhill running. This places great strain upon the inner surface of the kneecap and is a major cause of knee pain. There are two ways of avoiding this problem: one is to exercise in order to strengthen the thigh musculature and the other is simply to shun steep downhill stretches when training. Generally speaking, a steep uphill stretch can be good for the heart and lungs and the thigh and abdominal muscles, while a steep downhill section is of no use to anyone.

Common problems

Some common problems can occur for reasons which at first sight seem unlikely. In Chapter 3 we looked at the difficulties of running in cold conditions (see pages 89 – 91). Cold damp weather certainly does increase the chances of your suffering injury, but usually the selection of suitable clothing is an adequate preventative measure. A second factor can be the time of day: there are more injuries to athletes training in the early morning, because of stiffness. Other superficially unlikely factors in this context are lack of sleep and stress at work or at home, any or all of which can lead to a loss of your normal running rhythm and failure to notice unevenness in the running surface.

Knees: Although US surveys appear to show that pain around the knee is the most common type of running injury, my own experience belies this. Nevertheless, knee-related injuries are important. The pain may be the result of the soft tissues being stretched or, as we have seen, of abnormal wear on the inner surface of the kneecap.

If you are suffering from knee pains, you should have your legs checked to make sure that they are of equal length and that your thigh muscles are of equal strength. As noted, you may be running with your feet turned too far outwards (in which case, examine your arm action). Check the shock absorbency of your shoes, and think about the amount of downhill running you do.

If your knee becomes swollen, stop running and, until it settles, do only exercises to tighten the thigh muscles. The treatment may be speeded up through the use of contrast bathing. This consists of the application of hot and cold towels (or of hot water and ice in polythene bags) alternately. Allow one minute with the hot towel to three minutes with the cold, repeated three times. The whole procedure should be followed two or three times a day. Contrast bathing is also useful in the treatment of ankle and muscle strains, provided that you do not start the treatment until two days after incurring the injury.

If there is no swelling, then exercise the thigh muscles by, for example, stepping up onto a chair or beer-crate. Put the weak leg up on the chair first, and then use it to lift the body. Make sure that the knee of the weak leg straightens fully, and that there is no push-off from the strong leg. Hold the position for five seconds and then slowly lower yourself. You should run only as much as you can without causing yourself discomfort and, initially at least, your running should be on a level grassy surface.

Achilles tendon: Trouble with the Achilles tendon is very common. Should yours become sore then stop training *at once*. A few days' rest early on can save weeks or months of enforced rest later. There are a few, a very few, injuries which can successfully be 'run through', but Achilles-tendon problems are not among them.

To begin with, reduce the strain on the tendon by putting a pad of chiropody felt or foam in any shoe which you wear on the foot in question; often ultrasonic treatment by a physiotherapist is helpful. Do stretching exercises, and allow yourself to return only gradually to your training schedule. Occasionally an injection of hydrocortisone alongside the tendon or an operation may be required, but neither is a magic cure, and both involve definite risks.

It is worth trying to find out what caused the complaint in the first place, so that you can take measures to prevent it happening again. Check on the flexibility of your tendon. Have you recently changed your footwear from built-up heels to racing flats? Have you been going in for any unaccustomed hill work or sand running? Do you have worn-down heels on your shoes or flat feet inside them? Have you increased your training distances too much? These are some of the questions you should ask.

'*Shin splints*' is really a ragbag diagnosis covering several possible conditions. The most usual is tenderness, possibly with some swelling, on the inner aspect of the shin bone, the most sensitive area being just off the bone. Should it happen to you, check to make sure that you are not taking too long running strides, that you are not running with your feet turned outwards, and that you are not being affected by abnormal running surfaces. Treatment is by stretching the Achilles tendon and the calf muscles, thereby strengthening the muscles on the front part of the lower leg.

One condition which is definitely not included under the 'shin splints' umbrella is a stress fracture, a crack in the bone caused by repeated impacts such as those experienced in long-distance running. Here the tenderness is always on the bone itself. Diagnosis requires an X-ray, which will not show changes until two weeks after the start of the trouble.

Foot problems are numerous and important. Abnormalities of the foot may cause problems anywhere in the lower limbs or in the back. Readers with possible foot problems should consult the booklet *Athletes' Feet*, published by *Runners' World*.

General points

This chapter has covered a few of the problems which cause injuries to marathon runners; obviously there are many which have not been mentioned.

Different doctors have different ideas on treatment, so your best plan is to find one whom you can trust, and listen to his or her advice. If the problem does not solve itself, then by all means get a second opinion — but avoid falling into the trap of trailing your difficulty around several doctors until you find one who will give you the advice you want to hear. This is about as much use as having six training coaches and trying to follow all their routines at once.

Remember that you are a strange beast to want to run a marathon and to devote months or years to acquiring the ability to do so. Regrettably, some of your injuries may take months to cure, and you must display the same sort of patience as you do in your training. It is many weeks since I last witnessed a miracle.

6 Marathon facts and figures
Ron Holman

All sorts and conditions of marathoners

Age would appear to be of little significance to marathon runners.

The oldest man known to have completed a marathon was a Greek, Dimitrou Yordanidis, who ran the traditional route from Marathon to Athens in 7 hours 33 minutes in 1976 when he was 98 years old.

Jack Holden was over 42 when he won the Commonwealth title in 1950, and he ran the last 13km (8 miles) or so barefoot, having discarded his shoes because of blisters: he also survived an attack by a Great Dane 3km (2 miles) out from the finish. When he was 43 he added the European championship to his tally by beating the Finn, Veikko Karvonen, by over half a minute.

Karvonen's fellow countryman, Vaino Muinonen, after winning the European marathon in 1938 finished second eight years later when almost 47 years of age. Adolf Gruber of Austria won a record 12 national titles in the marathon between 1952 and 1963, the last at the age of 43. Sweden's oldest athletics champion was Erik Ostbye, who was almost 45 when he won the marathon in 1965.

Joyce Smith became the UK's oldest record holder when in 1981 she ran her first sub two-and-a-half-hour marathon, 22 years after winning her first national cross-country title. One year later, at the age of almost 45, she ran 2:29.43 to lower the record again, her seventh win in ten marathons.

Squire Yarrow, having finished second in the 1938 European marathon, won the AAA championship eight years later at the age of 41 and was placed seventh in that year's European championships. Mexico's Antonio Villaneuva ran 2:13.41 in the Nike-Oregon Track Club marathon in 1982 when over 40 years old. Jack Foster of New Zealand, who took up running in his 30s, won the silver medal in the 1974 Commonwealth Games with a time of 2:11.19 at the age of 42.

One need hardly add that persistence and determination are necessary qualities for the successful marathon runner. Mamo Wolde of Ethiopia struck

---

Joyce Smith (right) battles for the lead with Glynis Penny, a sub-2:46 marathon runner, in the British national 10-mile road championship

gold in the Olympics only at the third attempt: in 1956 he had finished last in his heat at both the 800m and the 1,500m; in 1964 he was fourth in the 10,000m; but he won the marathon in 1968 in the altitude of Mexico City and four years later was third in Munich.

Ron Hill was another athlete to demonstrate these qualities. In the European championships he dropped out in 1962 and finished twelfth in 1966, before going on to win a gold medal in 1969 on the difficult Athens course, and a bronze medal in 1971.

In 1966 during the Commonwealth marathon Jim Alder, running in the lead, was misdirected near the stadium. He curbed his shock at seeing a 70m lead over Bill Adcocks become a 30m deficit, overtook the Englishman, and won the gold medal for Scotland. He could have done with some local knowledge of the course — like France's first Olympic gold medallist, Michel Theato. In the 1900 Olympic marathon, held in Paris in temperatures of 39°C (102°F), Theato overcame the blistering conditions and used the knowledge he had acquired as a baker's roundsman to conquer the twisting route.

Paradoxically, the marathon can be the event for both the consistent veteran and the unranked newcomer. The 1978 Commonwealth champion, Gidemas Shahanga of Tanzania, was almost unknown, having been previously placed no higher than seventh, in the African Games. In the European championships the Belgian Aurele Vandendriesche won the silver medal in 1962 and 1966, finishing second to a UK runner on both occasions.

In these championships, the marathon has been the UK's most successful event, with a tally of five gold medals and a record total of ten overall medals at the distance. Belgium, too, has a good record in Europe: apart from Vandendriesche, Gaston Roelants, after a long cross-country and steeple-chase career, was placed second in 1969, fifth in 1971 and third in 1974, and his compatriot Karel Lismont was first in 1971, third in 1978 and third in 1982 as well as being placed second in the 1972 Olympics and third in the 1976 Olympics.

The USSR has two distinctions in the European event. A Russian runner provided the largest winning margin when Sergei Popov won in 2:15.17, a new world's best time, in 1958. Popov was 5 minutes 33.6 seconds clear of the second man. In 1978 the closest margin was supplied by Leonid Mosseyev when he beat his fellow Russian, Nikolay Penzin, by 1.5 seconds.

Consistency is another hallmark usually attributed to marathon runners. Certainly John J. Kelley demonstrated it: he won eight USA titles at the distance between 1956 and 1963. In the UK, Donald McNab Robertson took six AAA marathon championships, in 1932, 1933, 1934, 1936, 1937 and 1939.

New Zealand's Jack Foster

No one nation can claim a monopoly on marathon success. In the Introduction we noted the influence of Japan (see page 11), and its near neighbour Korea has also played a major part. In the 1932 Olympics Un-bal Kim was placed sixth; in 1936 Kitei Son, who took the gold medal for Japan, was actually Korean by birth, and Sung-yong Nam of Korea was third; in both 1952 and 1956 Korean runners were fourth. The Boston marathon was won by Koreans in 1947 (Yun Bok Suh) and 1950 (Kee Yong Ham), with the 1947 event being a clean sweep for Korea — first, second and third places. The trainer who accompanied the 1947 team was none other than Kitei Son, now known by his Korean name of Kee Chung Sohn.

Japan has provided the fastest marathoning twins. Shigeru Sou won the 1968 Beppu race in 2:09.05.6, beating brother Takeshi. Takeshi ran 2:09.49 for second place at Fukuoka in 1980 with Shigeru in fifth place. In the UK the Holt twins demonstrated remarkable similarities in a wide range of track times before David ran 2:16.53 and Robert recorded 2:16.50 for the marathon.

The classic events

Many countries now hold marathon races which have become classic events. The London marathon has recently entered this realm, but as a classic event was preceded in the UK by the Polytechnic marathon. This race was first held in 1909 from Windsor to Stamford Bridge, but in 1932 the finish point was changed to White City and later it was altered yet again to Chiswick; unfortunately, problems with traffic have now necessitated a circular route around Windsor. The race derives its name from the organisers, Polytechnic Harriers. The most wins in it have been recorded by Sam Ferris of the RAF, who made his marathon debut with second place in the 1924 event. Subsequently he achieved eight 'Poly' wins (1925 – 9 and 1931 – 3) and ran in three Olympic marathons, gaining fifth (1924), eighth (1928) and second (1932) places. Ferris won twelve of his nineteen marathons. Jim Peters also had a fine record in the Polytechnic marathon with four successive wins in the years 1951 – 4. In his first win he set a new British best time (2:29.24) and in each of the subsequent three years he set a new world's best (from 2:20.42.2 to 2:17.39.4).

In the USA the major rival to the New York marathon is the Boston event. This was first held in 1897, and is run each year in April in honour of Paul Revere's ride through the city. Its present route — Hopkinton to Boston's Prudential Centre — has been used since 1965. The race first had more than 1,000 competitors in 1968, and the numbers steadily climbed until the late 1970s when tighter qualifying standards were introduced and a closer watch kept for gatecrashers. In 1979 there was an official record field of 7,877 runners with, in addition to this, more than 2,000 runners who started unofficially: the average number of starters is still over 6,000.

John Kelley has run in almost every Boston marathon since 1928. He won the race in 1935 and again ten years later. In 1982 he ran in his 51st Boston marathon at the age of 74.

The record number of Boston wins is a total of seven by Clarence de Mar, with three in succession in the years 1922–4. Three successive wins were not recorded again until Bill Rodgers emulated de Mar between 1978 and 1980. Rodgers owns a running-gear shop located at the 22-mile point on the Boston course.

Rodgers also has the record number of wins in the New York marathon, finishing first four times in a row from 1976 (when he ran his fastest time for the course of 2:10.10) to 1979. The following year, Alberto Salazar made his astonishing debut at the distance to win in 2:09.41; he lowered this further the next year to set a new world's best of 2:08.13. After the succession of record-breaking wins by Grete Waitz, the women's record was set in 1981 by Alison Roe of New Zealand.

Another popular course for marathon runners is the Fukuoka event which is held in Japan each year in early December. The course is flat and fast.

Bill Rodgers

Alberto Salazar (wearing no. 3) in the 1981 New York marathon

This is where Derek Clayton set a world's best time (2:09.36.4) in 1967 which remained a course record until 1981 when Robert De Castella, also of Australia and currently the Commonwealth champion, ran 2:08.18 — only five seconds short of Salazar's world's-best time (see frontispiece). Toshihika Seto of Japan and Jerome Drayton of Canada have both won the event three times, but Frank Shorter holds the record with four wins between 1971 and 1974. Fukuoka has also provided a depth of field in terms of world-class times: seven runners had times faster than 2 hours 20 minutes in 1962, 11 in 1964, and 29 in 1975.

Even better than the Japanese event in this respect was the US Olympic trial in 1980. Tony Sandoval won in 2:10.19, leading home an amazing 56 men before 2 hours and 20 minutes was up. The following year in Boston even this was surpassed when 64 men beat this time. On the same day as the US trial race, the Soviet championship was held in Moscow: this produced 52 men with times under 2:20, led home by Vladimir Kotov in 2:10.58.

Table 22 *Marathon times*

	hours : minutes				
Number of runners under	2:20	2:30	2:40	2:50	3:00
Boston 1981	64	297	857	1,788	2,840
New York 1981	49	186	420	848	1,603
London 1981	17	144	406	770	1,294

Professional marathoners

Surprisingly, even indoor marathons have been run. Johnny Nylen of Sweden ran 2:28.09 in Goteborg in 1979. As a professional runner, Viljami Kolehmainen had run 2:29.39.2 in an event in 1912 which actually took place on a running track. After the 1908 Olympics a series of professional races were run in the USA; the runners included the Olympic champion John Hayes, Tom Longboat (a Canadian Indian), Alfred Shrubb (from England), and Italy's Dorando Pietri. Venues included Madison Square Garden and the New York Polo Ground; in the last event held here the winner's prize money — taken by a 40—1 outsider — was $10,000.

In 1980 professionalism again emerged with a marathon at Atlantic City, New Jersey, for men and women in which the first-place prize money was set at $15,000. Currently there is the Association of Road Racing Athletes in the USA promoting road races, including marathons. The biggest prize money so far offered was the $25,000 won in Los Angeles in 1981 by Tom Fleming (2:13.15) and Cindy Dalrymple (2:39.33).

Runners before (above) *and after* (below) *the New York marathon*

Faster and faster

Women had a long, hard fight for acceptance in the marathon, despite the fact that a Greek woman unofficially finished the 1896 Olympic event in about four and a half hours. In 1964, Dale Greig of the UK was the first woman to run inside three and a half hours, on the tough Isle of Wight course. It was seven years before a further thirty minutes were clipped from this time — Adrienne Beames of Australia achieved this when she ran 2:46.30 in her home country. The first championship for women was held in the USA in 1970. The previously mentioned Waldniel international race (see page 19) first took place in 1974.

At the top level in marathon running, the number of competitors running faster than 2:20 increased in the years 1960—70 from 12 to 103. Five years later this figure had become 148. Marathon races in the USA alone more than trebled in this period, to a total of 148 by 1975.

On this page and the next, in Tables 23, 24 and 25, you will find marathon running's 'roll of honour' — the winners of the Olympic, European Championship and Commonwealth Games events.

Table 23 *Olympic marathon winners*

1896	April 10	Athens	Spiridon Louis (Greece)	2:58:50
1900	July 19	Paris	Michel Theato (France)	2:59:45
1904	August 30	St Louis	Thomas Hicks (USA)	3:28:53
1908	July 24	London	John Hayes (USA)	2:55:18.4
1912	July 14	Stockholm	Kenneth McArthur (South Africa)	2:36:54.8
1920	August 22	Antwerp	Hannes Kolehmainen (Finland)	2:32:35.8
1924	July 13	Paris	Albin Stenroos (Finland)	2:41:22.6
1928	August 5	Amsterdam	Mohammed el Ouafi (France)	2:32:57
1932	August 7	Los Angeles	Juan Carlos Zabala (Argentina)	2:31:36
1936	August 9	Berlin	Kitei Son (Japan)	2:29:19.2
1948	August 7	London	Delfo Cabrera (Argentina)	2:34:51.6
1952	July 27	Helsinki	Emil Zatopek (Czechoslovakia)	2:23:03.2
1956	December 1	Melbourne	Alain Mimoun (France)	2:25:00
1960	September 10	Rome	Abebe Bikila (Ethiopia)	2:15:16.2
1964	October 21	Tokyo	Abebe Bikila (Ethiopia)	2:12:11.2
1968	October 20	Mexico City	Mamo Wolde (Ethiopia)	2:20:26.4
1972	September 19	Munich	Frank Shorter (USA)	2:12:19.8
1976	July 31	Montreal	Waldemar Cierpinski (East Germany)	2:09:55
1980	August 1	Moscow	Waldemar Cierpinski (East Germany)	2:11:03

Table 24 *European Championship marathon winners*

1934	September 9	Turin	Armas Toivonen (Finland)	2:52:29
1938	September 4	Paris	Vaino Muinonen (Finland)	2:37:28.8
1946	August 22	Oslo	Mikko Hietanen (Finland)	2:24:55
				(short course)
1950	August 23	Brussels	Jack Holden (Great Britain)	2:32:13.2
1954	August 25	Berne	Veikko Karvonen (Finland)	2:24:51.6
1958	August 24	Stockholm	Sergei Popov (USSR)	2:15:17
1962	September 16	Belgrade	Brian Kilby (Great Britain)	2:23:18.8
1966	September 4	Budapest	Jim Hogan (Great Britain)	2:20:04.6
1969	September 21	Athens	Ron Hill (Great Britain)	2:16:47.8
1971	August 15	Helsinki	Karel Lismont (Belgium)	2:13:09
1974	September 8	Rome	Ian Thompson (Great Britain)	2:13:18.8
1978	September 3	Prague	Leonid Mosseyev (USSR)	2:11:57.5
1982	September 12	Athens	Gerard Nijboer (Holland)	2:15:16
1982*	September 12	Athens	Rosa Mota (Portugal)	2:36:03.9

* Inaugural women's race.

Table 25 *Commonwealth Games marathon winners*

1930	August 23	Hamilton	Duncan Wright (Scotland)	2:43:43
1934	August 11	London	Harold Webster (Canada)	2:40:36
1938	February 12	Sydney	Johannes Coleman (South Africa)	2:30:49.8
1950	February 11	Auckland	Jack Holden (England)	2:32:57
1954	August 7	Vancouver	Joe McGhee (Scotland)	2:39:36
1958	July 24	Cardiff	Dave Power (Australia)	2:22:45.6
1962	November 29	Perth	Brian Kilby (England)	2:21:17
1966	August 11	Kingston	Jim Alder (Scotland)	2:22:07.8
1970	July 23	Edinburgh	Ron Hill (England)	2:09:28
1974	January 31	Christchurch	Ian Thompson (England)	2:09:12
1978	August 11	Edmonton	Gidemas Shahanga (Tanzania)	2:15:40
1982	October 8	Brisbane	Robert De Castella (Australia)	2:09:18

But what about you?

If you are now convinced that you want to run a marathon, the best advice that we can give you is to join an athletics club. Although we feel that the advice we have given in this book is sound and based on scientific principles, membership of a club brings other advantages — such as the fellowship of other runners, access to races other than marathons which could be an important part of your preparation, and the possibility of contact with a qualified and experienced distance-running coach. It can be invaluable to have the company of others to train with (provided, of course, that they are

Runners in the 1982 Witney 12-mile road race. It can be an important part of your preparation to take part in races other than marathons

of a similar standard to yourself), and also to know someone who can discuss, direct and personally tailor the guidelines given in this book to your own needs and circumstances.

Your local public library should have the addresses of athletic clubs in your area. In case of difficulty, you can contact your area athletic association. A list of these is given in Appendix 1 (page 143).

Once you have joined a suitable club, we are sure that you will become as avid as virtually every other distance runner to read as much as possible about your sport. As well as the periodicals published by the organisations we have listed in Appendix 2 (page 143), there are many other magazines and books worth reading: you will find a selection of these on pages 155 – 156.

Many of the magazines contain details of where you can buy your running kit, either by direct purchase or by mail order. Although it is sometimes false economy to buy cheap kit, track suits which are perfectly serviceable are now available from many of the larger chain stores at prices often lower than those in the specialist shops. Against that, many sports-goods shops are now run by people who are athletes themselves, so that good advice as to your most suitable purchase comes free. However, do remember

Buy a good pair of shoes, to help avoid injury

that the store is primarily a business: in the USA one running-gear retailer, which had one store in 1972, had 410 at the last count; and a major sports-shoe company which in the same year had a revenue of 1.7 million dollars had increased that by 1981 to 185 million dollars.

Certainly it is imperative that you buy a good pair of shoes — each of your feet hits the road about 1,000 times every mile (625 times per kilometre), and as it lands the peak force is three times your body weight. Do not use plimsolls or tennis or squash shoes, which are not designed for running or for the surfaces that you will be running on. Remember to try on *both* shoes before you buy, and move around in them to check that they are comfortable.

If you should be unfortunate enough to sustain an injury, follow the advice given in Chapter 5. If the injury persists after appropriate first-aid treatment, see your doctor as soon as possible and, if he cannot treat you, obtain a letter of referral to a Sports Injury Clinic. Some of those in major city centres in the UK are listed in Appendix 3, and in Appendix 4 you will find information about physiotherapists who specialise in the treatment of sports injuries.

We hope that the information and advice we have given in this book will enhance your enjoyment of the greatest athletic event of all — the marathon.

Appendices

Appendix 1 *Area Athletic Associations in the UK*

Northern Counties AAA
Studio 44, Bluecoat Chambers
School Lane
Liverpool L1 3BR
Telephone 051-708 9363

Midland Counties AAA
Devonshire House
High Street
Deritend
Birmingham B12 0LP
Telephone 021-773 1631

Southern Counties AAA
Francis House
Francis Street
London SW1P 1DL
Telephone 01-828 9326

Scottish AAA
16 Royal Crescent
Glasgow G3 7SL
Telephone 041-332 5144

Northern Ireland AAA
20 Kernan Park
Portadown
Co. Armagh
Northern Ireland BT63 5QY
Telephone 0762 34652

Welsh AAA
Winterbourne
Greenway Close
Llandough
Penarth
South Glamorgan CF6 1LZ
Telephone 0222 708102

Where the women's associations are at different addresses from those listed above we are sure that any enquiries will be redirected. The governing body for women's road running in the UK is the Women's Cross-Country Association, 10 Anderton Close, Bury, BL8 2HQ, Lancashire.

Appendix 2 *Specialist Clubs in the UK*

Once you are a member of an athletics club, there are a number of specialist clubs you may wish to join.

The Road Runners' Club was founded in 1952 and is concerned not only with marathon running but with all road races longer than 10 miles (16km). You must be a member of an athletics club affiliated to either the AAA or Women's AAA (both housed at the same address as the Southern Counties AAA) before you can join.

Membership of the RRC entitles you to a regular newsletter with results from all over the world, interesting articles and a fixture list. The club also runs a worthwhile and reasonable insurance scheme which covers accidents while training or racing. The Honorary Secretary is Don Turner, 40 Rosedale Road, Stoneleigh, Epsom, Surrey, KT17 2JH.

The British Marathon Runners' Club (Membership Secretary: Dick Hughes, 5 Priory Close, Deeping St Mary, Peterborough) is restricted to British runners who have achieved the following times:

Men Senior 3hr; Veterans (40−49 years) 3hr 15min; (50−59 years) 3hr 40min; (60-plus) 4hr.

Women Senior 3hr 30min; Veterans (35−49 years) 3hr 40min; (50-plus) 4hr.

The BMRC publishes a useful annual handbook, and organises occasional seminars, training days, etc.

The London Road Runners' Club, 6 Upper Montague Street, London W1 (Tel.: 01-723 4379), was founded in 1980. There are no restrictions on membership and the club promotes a number of races in the London area including one held on New Year's Eve in Battersea Park.

Marathon Club UK, 51−67 Bryan Street, Hanley, Stoke-on-Trent (Tel.: 0782 263850). This newly formed organisation places no restriction on membership and provides advice and information on all aspects of marathon running. It publishes annually the *Marathon Guide* which lists practically every road race, including marathons, held in the UK.

Appendix 3 *Sports injury clinics in the UK*

Aldershot

Cambridge Military Hospital
Aldershot
Hampshire GU11 2AN
Telephone 0252 22521 (ext. 208)

Bedford

Bedford General Hospital
Kimbolton Road
Bedford MK10 2NU
Telephone 0234 55122

Birmingham

Accident Hospital
Bath Row
Birmingham B15 1NA
Telephone 021-643 7041

General Hospital
Steelhouse Lane
Birmingham B4 6NH
Telephone 021-236 8611

Bristol

Royal Infirmary
Marlborough Street
Bristol BS2 8HW
Telephone 0272 22041

Cambridge
Addenbrooke's Hospital
Hills Road
Cambridge CB2 2QQ
Telephone 0223 45151 (ext. 254)

Colchester
Severalls Hospital
Mile End
Colchester
Essex CO4 5HG
Telephone 0206 77271

Derby
Royal Infirmary
London Road
Derby DE1 2QY
Telephone 0332 47141 (ext. 556)

Glasgow
Victoria Infirmary
Langside
Glasgow G42 9TY
Telephone 041-649 4545

Guildford
St Luke's Hospital
Warren Road
Guildford
Surrey GU1 3NT
Telephone 0483 71122

Haywards Heath
Cuckfield Hospital
Cuckfield
Sussex RH17 5HQ
Telephone 0444 459122

Leeds
St James' University Hospital
Beckett Street
Leeds LS9 7TF
Telephone 0532 433144

London
Guy's Hospital
St Thomas Street
London SE1 9RT
Telephone 01-407 7600 (ext. 2424)

Kings College Hospital
Denmark Hill
London SE5 9RS
Telephone 01-274 6222 (ext. 2434)

Middlesex Hospital
Mortimer Street
London W1N 8AA
Telephone 01-636 8333

Westminster Hospital
Dean Ryle Street
London SW1P 2AP
Telephone 01-828 9811

Hillingdon Hospital
Uxbridge
Middlesex 4B8 3NN
Telephone 01-893 8282

St Charles' Hospital
Exmoor Street
London W10 6DZ
Telephone 01-969 2488

Royal Northern Hospital
Holloway Road
London N7 6LD
Telephone 01-272 7777

Hackney Hospital
Homerton High Street
London E9 6BE
Telephone 01-985 5555

Crystal Palace National Sports Centre
London SE19 2BB
Telephone 01-778 0131

Northampton
General Hospital
Billing Road
Northampton NN1 5BD
Telephone 0604 34700

Slough
Farnham Park Rehabilitation Centre
Farnham Royal
Slough
Buckinghamshire SL2 3LR
Telephone 02814 2271

Appendix 4 *The Association of Chartered Physiotherapists in Sports Medicine*

Aims: The aims of the Association of Chartered Physiotherapists in Sports Medicine are:

A: to improve the techniques and facilities for the treatment of sports injuries;

B: to inform all interested bodies of the availability of such specialised treatment by physiotherapists.

The association produces a directory which lists the names of all chartered physiotherapists who have a special interest in the treatment of sports injuries. Any enquiries may be directed to the Honorary Secretary: David Chapman, White Oaks Clinic, Heathfield, Sussex, TN21 8UN Tel: Heathfield (04352) 3694 and 4545. The secretary can also give information to clubs and other concerned parties about courses run by the association, as well as providing a list of those chartered physiotherapists who would be willing to give outside lectures.

Appendix 5 *Training Diaries*

The only way in which you can keep a personal record of your own times in particular races is by the use of a training diary. This is also useful to chart your day-by-day training — hopefully over the course of months and years. By referring back to your diary, mistakes such as building up your training distances too quickly, racing too often, or having insufficient rest between training sessions may be seen and rectified for the future.

On page 147 we reproduce an extract from the training diary of Gerard Nijboer of Holland dating from shortly before he won the Amsterdam marathon in 1980. Nijboer went on to win the silver medal in the Moscow Olympics the same year, and in 1982 won the European marathon in Athens.

As you can see, this extract records the distances run and the pace of the training sessions, together with the components that make up each of them. However, training diaries or logs can be much more detailed, containing notes of personal feelings before, during and after the run, with details of the course and of training partners also recorded.

Monday	am	7 miles (11.2km) at 9mph (14.4kph) pace
	pm	13 miles (20.8km) including 10 × 1,000m in 3 minutes run on track
Tuesday	am	8 miles (12.8km) at 8−9mph (12.8−14.4kph) pace
	pm	12½ miles (20km) including 2 × 15 minutes' fast
Wednesday	am	5 miles (8km) at 8−9mph (12.8−14.4kph) pace
	pm	18½ miles (29.6km) at 8−9mph (12.8−14.4kph) pace
Thursday	pm	13 miles (20.8km) including 3 × 10 minutes' fast
Friday	am	7 miles (11.2km) at 10mph (16kph) pace
	pm	9 miles (14.4km) at 10¾mph (17.2kph) pace
Saturday	am	17 miles' (27.2km) fartlek
Sunday	am	5 miles (8km) at 8½mph (13.6kph) pace
	pm	5½ miles (8.8km) cross-country and road race (28.03)

This next extract is from the training log of Nick Brawn, an English cross-country international runner, and represents the week of training which led up to his marathon debut in New York in 1981.

Sunday	am	15 miles (24km) steady (1½ hours) over road and trails
Monday	am	6 miles (9.6km) steady road and country (35 minutes) plus stretching
	pm	20 × 200m in 31.4 seconds average, with 200m jogs between in 1 minute
Tuesday	am	10 miles (16km) steady on road (58 minutes 16 seconds)
Wednesday	am	7 miles (11.2km) steady (45 minutes) cross-country and road
Thursday	pm	5½ miles (8.8km) easy (35 minutes) plus stretching
Friday	pm	5 miles (8km) quite easy (approximately 30 minutes)
Saturday	am	4 miles (6.4km) — 2 miles (3.2km) jog; 2 miles (3.2km) jog and strides
Sunday		New York Marathon. 4th. 2:11.09.

Nick Brawn records much more detail than this in his training log — e.g., his morning pulse count, a weekly weight check, his hours of sleep and the weather conditions. For example, we learn from his diary that on the day of the race the temperature was 11°C (52°F) with a breeze. His weight was slightly above average — he had just finished the second half of a carbo-hydrate-boosting diet — and his pulse was also slightly raised, almost certainly due to nervous anticipation of the race.

Nick Brawn keeps very detailed entries in his training log

These diary extracts have not been included for you to copy — you must remember that both of these runners are world-class athletes — but to indicate to you how useful a training diary can be in logging your marathon career.

Harry Wilson, British middle-distance event coach and mentor to Steve Ovett and many other international runners, describes a training diary as a book to study when planning future seasons. It can provide clues to success and failure, and it is an essential record to show to a coach when asking for advice.

Below we list three commercially produced training diaries which are currently available in the UK. Some runners prefer to use a more normal type of desk or pocket diary, but we feel that those we have listed provide certain advantages.

Arena Training Diary. Costs £1.10 (1982) and lasts 18 months. Contains graphs for training pace, etc. Spaces for weather conditions, training conditions, daily pulse and weight records as well as general comments. Fits into a suit or jacket pocket. Obtainable from Arena Publications, 325 High Road, London SW16 3NS.

Runners' Training Diary. Lasts one year. Contains performance, mileage and weight graphs. Space provided for a personal fixture list. Useful foreword by UK coach Harry Wilson. Priced at £2 (1982) and obtainable from Flintbarn Ltd., The Sport Spot, 171 Hatfield Road, St. Albans, Hertfordshire AL1 4LB.

Runners' Log. Introduction by Bill Rodgers. Stretching programme for flexibility by Bob Anderson. Progress charts and race-record page. Available at £3.25 (1982) from *Running* Magazine, PO Box 50, Market Harborough, Leicestershire. (Allow 21 days for delivery.)

Appendix 6 *BAAB Senior Coaches for the Marathon*

J. Kennedy
'Fern Hill', 43 Long Causeway
Monk Bretton
Barnsley
Yorkshire S71 2JB

T. Shrimpton
9 New Zealand Avenue
Salisbury
Wiltshire SP2 7JX

A. Storey
14 Willowtree Avenue
Gilesgate Moor
Durham DH1 1EB

Dr J. H. L. Humphreys
55 The Drive
Alwoodley
Leeds LS17 7QG

J. B. Howcroft
48 Squires Lane
Tyldesley
Manchester M29 8JF

C. Daley
12 Plane Street
Rhydefelin
Pontypridd
Mid-Glamorgan CF37 5DE

D. Shelley
22 Mount Avenue
Stone
Staffordshire ST15 8HU

E. G. Austin
58 Belmont Street
Worcester SR3 8NN

References

CHAPTER 1

Burenkov, S. P., and Glasunov, I. S.: 'USSR: the preventive approach in public health', *World Health Forum*, Vol. 3 No. 1, 1982 (pp. 54−7)

Ciba Foundation: 'Prevention of coronary heart disease in the United Kingdom', *Lancet*, Vol. 1 No. 8276, April 10, 1982

Cooper, K.H., Pollock, M.L., Martin, R.P., White, S.R., Linnerud, A.C., and Jackson, A.: 'Physical fitness levels *vs* selected coronary risk factors; a cross-sectional study', *Journal of the American Medical Association*, Vol. 236 No. 2, July 12, 1976

Costill, D. L.: 'Physiology of marathon running', *Journal of the American Medical Association*, Vol. 221 No. 9, August 28, 1972

Costill, D. L.: *A Scientific Approach to Distance Running*, Tafnews (USA), 1979

Hampton, J. R.: 'Falling mortality in coronary heart disease', *British Medical Journal*, Vol. 284 No. 6328, May 22, 1982

Hartnung, G. H., Foreyk, J. P., Mitchell, R. E., Vlasek, I., and Gotho, A. M.: 'Relation of diet to high-density lipoprotein cholesterol in middle-aged marathon runners, joggers and inactive men', *New England Journal of Medicine*, Vol. 302 No. 7, February 14, 1980

Haycock, C. E.: 'Sports medicine', *Journal of the American Medical Association*, Vol. 247 No. 21, June 4, 1982

Heneson, N.: 'How to eat, drink and avoid cancer', *New Scientist*, Vol. 95 No. 1258, June 17, 1982

Lambert, C. A., Netherton, D. R., Finison, L. J., Hyde, J. N., and Spaight, S. J.: 'Risk factors and life style: a state-wide health interview survey', *New England Journal of Medicine*, Vol. 306 No. 17, April 29, 1982

Levin, D. C.: 'The runner's high: fact or fiction?', *Journal of the American Medical Association*, Vol. 248 No. 1, July 2, 1982

McKie, R.: 'Warning: exercise can seriously damage your health', *Observer*, August 29, 1982

MacLennan, Sir H.: 'The meaning of physical fitness', *Proceedings of the Royal Society of Medicine*, Vol. 62, November, 1979

Margaria, R.: 'The sources of muscular energy', *Scientific American*, March, 1972

Miller, G. J., and Miller, N. E.: 'Plasma high-density lipoprotein concentration and development of ischaemic heart disease', *Lancet*, Vol. 1 No. 7897, January 4, 1975

Milvy, P.: 'Statistical analysis of deaths from coronary heart disease in a cohort of marathon runners', *Annals of New York Academy of Sciences*, Vol. 301, 1977

Morris, J. N., Adam, C., Chave, S. P. W., Sirey, C., Epstein, L., and Sheehan, D. G.: 'Vigorous exercise in leisure-time and the incidence of coronary heart disease', *Lancet*, Vol. 1 No. 7799, February 17, 1973

Strasser, T.: 'Coronary risk factors revisited', *World Health Forum*, Vol. 3 No. 1, 1982

Varnauskas, E., Bergman, H., Hauk, P., and Bjorntoop, P.: 'Haemodynamic effects of physical training in coronary patients', *Lancet*, Vol. 2 No. 7453, July 2, 1966

Vener, A. M., Krupka, L. R., and Gerard, R. J.: 'Overweight/obese patients: an overview', *The Practitioner*, Vol. 226, June, 1982

Williams, P. T., Wood, P. D., Haskell, W. L., and Vranizan, K.: 'The effects of running mileage and duration on plasma lipoprotein levels', *Journal of the American Medical Association*, Vol. 247 No. 19, May 21, 1982

Wood, C.: 'Europe looks at heart disease', *New Scientist*, Vol. 95 No. 1256, June 3, 1982

CHAPTER 2

American College of Sports Medicine: *Guidelines for Graded Exercise Testing and Exercise Prescription* (2nd edn.), Lea and Febiger, Philadelphia, 1980 (pp. 12−14)

American Heart Association: *Exercise Testing and Training of Individuals with Heart Disease or at High Risk for its Development: A Handbook for Physicians*, American Heart Association, 1975 (p. 44)

Åstrand, P. O., and Rodahl, K.: *Textbook of Work Physiology* (2nd edn.), McGraw-Hill, New York, 1977

Burke, E., and Humphreys, J. H. L.: *Fit to Exercise*, Pelham, London, 1982

Cooper, K. H.: *The Aerobics Way*, Corgi, London, 1982

Costill, D. L.: 'Physiology of marathon running', *Journal of the American Medical Association*, Vol. 221 No. 9, August 28, 1972

Costill, D. L.: *A Scientific Approach to Distance Running*, Tafnews (USA), 1979

Costill, D. L.: *What Research Tells the Coach About Distance Running*, American Association for Health, Physical Education and Recreation, Washington, 1968

Costill, D. L., and Fox, E. L.: 'Energetics of marathon running', *Medicine and Science in Sport*, Vol. 1 No. 2, June, 1969 (pp. 81−6)

Daniels, J., Fitts, R., and Sheehan, G.: *Conditioning for Distance Running*, Wiley, New York, 1978

de Vries, H.: *Physiology of Exercise for Physical Education and Athletics* (3rd edn.), Wm. C. Brown, Iowa, 1980

Falls, H. B.: *Exercise Physiology*, Academic Press, New York, 1968

Fox, E. L.: *The Physiological Basis of Physical Education and Athletics* (3rd edn.), Saunders College Publishing, Philadelphia, 1981

Fox, E. L.: *Sports Physiology*, W. B. Saunders, Philadelphia, 1979

Fox, E. L., and Mathews, D. K.: *Interval Training*, W. B. Saunders, Philadelphia, 1974

Humphreys, J. H. L.: 'Training principles for marathon runners', *Athletics Coach*, Vol. 15 No. 3, September, 1981

Jensen, C. R.: *Scientific Basis of Athletic Conditioning* (2nd edn.), Lea and Febiger, Philadelphia, 1979

Karpovich, P. V.: *Physiology of Muscular Activity* (7th edn.), W. B. Saunders, Philadelphia, 1971

Morehouse, L. E., and Miller, A. T.: *Physiology of Exercise* (7th edn.),
    C. V. Mosby, Saint Louis, 1976
MacDougall, D., and Sale, D.: 'Continuous versus interval training: a review for
    the athlete and the coach', *Canadian Journal of Applied Sport Science*,
    1981 (pp. 93 – 7)
Pollock, M. L., Wilmore, J. H., and Fox, S. M.: *Health and Fitness Through
    Physical Activity*, Wiley, New York, 1978
Sharkey, B. J.: *Physiology of Fitness*, Human Kinetics Publishers, Illinois, 1979
Wilmore, J. H.: *Athletic Training and Physical Fitness*, Allyn and Bacon, 1976
Wilmore, J. H. (ed.): *Exercises and Sports Sciences Reviews*, Vol. 1,
    Academic Press, London, 1973
Williams, C.: 'Effects of endurance training', *Modern Athlete and Coach*,
    Vol. 14 No. 1, Adelaide, 1976

CHAPTER 3

Arendt, J., and Marks, V.: 'Physiological changes underlying jet lag',
    British Medical Journal, Vol. 284, January 16, 1982
Bergström, J., and Hultman, E.: 'Nutrition', *Journal of the American Medical
    Association*, Vol. 221 No. 9, August 28, 1972
Burch, G. E., and Giles, T. D.: 'A perspective on climate and man's health',
    Journal of the American Medical Association, Vol. 221 No. 9,
    August 28, 1972
Buskirk, E. R., and Bass, D. E.: *Science and Medicine of Exercise and Sport*,
    Harper and Row, New York, 1974
Costill, D. L.: *A Scientific Approach to Distance Running*, Tafnews (USA), 1979
Dick, F. W.: 'Relevance of altitude training', *Athletics Coach*, Vol. 13 No. 4,
    December, 1979
Finkel, A. J.: 'Do air pollution effects outweigh benefits of highway jogging?',
    Journal of the American Medical Association, Vol. 219 No. 9,
    February 28, 1972
Fox, E. L.: *Sports Physiology*, W. B. Saunders, Philadelphia, 1979
Holman, R.: 'Altitude training', *Athletics Coach*, Vol. 13 No. 4, December, 1979
Holman, R., and Dick, F. W.: 'Adaptation to heat', *Athletics Coach*, Vol. 16 No. 3,
    September, 1982
Lowe, D. D., and Caffrey, G. P.: 'Heat illnesses: prevention, symptoms and
    first aid care', in *Relevant Topics in Athletic Training* (ed. Burke and Scriber),
    Mouvement Publications, New York, 1977
Mirkin, G.: 'The perils of pollution', *The Runner*, June, 1980
Mirkin, G.: 'Running and smoking', *The Runner*, June, 1979
Selson, M.: 'Physiological changes underlying jet lag', *British Medical Journal*,
    Vol. 284, March 6, 1982
Sharp, N.C.C.: 'Some aspects of contemporary physiology applied to sports
    training methods', *Athletics Coach*, Vol. 14 No. 1, March, 1980
Shepherd, R. J.: *The Fit Athlete*, Oxford University Press, 1978
Shepherd, R. J.: 'Heart and circulation', *Journal of the American Medical
    Association*, Vol. 205 No. 11, September 9, 1968

Siekevitz, P., and Frederick, J. (eds.): *Conference on the Marathon: Physiological, Medical, Epidemiological and Psychological Studies*, New York Academy of Sciences, October 25—28, 1978

Stiles, M.: 'Medical preparation for the Olympics', *Journal of the American Medical Association*, Vol. 205 No. 11, September 9, 1968

Zuti, W. B.: 'Heat stress, conditioning and acclimatisation', in *Toward an Understanding of Human Performance* (ed. E. J. Burke), Mouvement Publications, New York, 1978

CHAPTER 4

Åstrand, P. O.: 'Diet and athletic performance', *Federation Proceedings*, Vol. 26 No. 6, November—December, 1967

Åstrand, P. O.: 'Food, nutrition and health', *World Review of Nutrition and Dietetics* (ed. M. Rechcigl), Vol. 16, 1973 (pp. 59—79)

Burke, E., and Humphreys, J. H. L.: *Fit to Exercise*, Pelham, London, 1982

Costill, D. L.: *A Scientific Approach to Distance Running*, Tafnews (USA), 1979

Costill, D. L.: 'Nutritional requirements for endurance athletes', in *Toward an Understanding of Human Performance* (ed. E. J. Burke), Mouvement Publications, New York, 1978

Costill, D. L.: 'Physiology of marathon running', *Journal of the American Medical Association*, Vol. 221 No. 9, August, 1972 (pp. 1024—9)

Costill, D. L., and Miller, J. M.: 'Nutrition for endurance sport: carbohydrate and fluid balance', *International Journal of Sports Medicine*, Vol. 1, 1980 (pp. 2—14)

Daniels, J., Fitts, R., and Sheehan, G.: *Conditioning for Distance Running (The Scientific Aspects)*, John Wiley & Sons, New York, 1978

Darden, E.: *Nutrition for Athletes*, Anna Publishing, Florida, 1978

de Vries, H. A.: *Physiology of Exercise for Physical Education and Athletics* (3rd edn.), W. C. Brown, Iowa, 1980

Fox, E. L.: *Sports Physiology*, W. B. Saunders, Philadelphia, 1979

Fox, E. L., and Mathews, D. K.: *The Physiological Basis of Physical Education and Athletics* (2nd edn.), Saunders College Publishing, Philadelphia, 1981

Humphreys, J.: 'Muscle glycogen loading (supercompensation for distance runners)', *Athletics Coach*, Vol. 13 No. 3, September, 1979

Jenson, C. R., and Fisher, A. G.: *Scientific Basis of Athletic Conditioning* (2nd edn.), Lea & Febiger, Philadelphia, 1979

Katch, F. I., and McArdle, W. D.: *Nutrition, Weight Control and Exercise*, Houghton Mifflin Company, Boston, 1977

McArdle, W. D., Katch, F. I., and Katch, V. L.: *Exercise Physiology (Energy, Nutrition and Human Performance)*, Lea & Febiger, Philadelphia, 1981

Maron, M. B., and Horvath, S. M.: 'The marathon: a history and review of the literature', *Medicine and Science in Sports*, Vol. 10 No. 2, 1978 (pp. 137—50)

National Dairy Council: 'Nutritional and athletic performance', *Relevant Topics for Athletic Training* (ed. K. Scriber and E. Burke), Mouvement Publications, New York, 1978

Parizkova, J., and Rogozkin, V. A. (eds.): *Nutrition, Physical Fitness and Health*, University Park Press, Baltimore, 1978

Smith, N. J.: 'Nutrition and the athlete', *Sports Medicine and Physiology* (ed. R. H. Strauss), W. B. Saunders, Philadelphia, 1979

Unitas, J., and Dintiman, G. (eds.): *Improving Health and Performance in the Athlete*, Prentice-Hall International, New Jersey, 1979
Wagner, B.: 'Nutrition in athletics', in *Toward an Understanding of Human Performance* (ed. E. Burke), Mouvement Publications, New York, 1978

CHAPTER 5

Armour, W. I., and Colsen, J. H.: *Sports Injuries and their Treatment*, Stanley Paul, 1982
Brady, D. M.: *Running Injuries*, Ciba Laboratories, 1981
Hlavac, H. F.: *The Foot Book*, Runners' World, 1979
Sheehan, G.: *Medical Advice for Runners*, Runners' World, 1981

CHAPTER 6

Much of the factual information contained in this chapter was drawn from:
Matthews, P.: *The Guinness Book of Athletics Facts and Feats*, Guinness Superlatives, London, 1982
(The authors are grateful to Guinness Superlatives for allowing them to use material from their book.)

Further reading

MAGAZINES

Athletics Weekly, 344 High Street, Rochester, Kent
Gives full coverage to all major events, results, news of forthcoming fixtures and the occasional training article. Most promoters advertise their road races, including marathons, with full entry details in this magazine.

Marathon and Distance Runner, Peterson House, Droitwich, Worcestershire
Incorporates the British Marathon Runners' Club *Newsletter*. Contains a good column by the 'Running Doctor' on medical and injury problems.

Marathoner, Box 366, Mountain View, California 94042
Quarterly journal published by World Publications, who issue also *Runners' World* (see below). Excellent reference material for the serious student of the event.

The Runner, One Park Avenue, New York, NY 10016 (Circulation office: Box 2730, Boulder, Colorado 80322)
Immaculately produced with excellent articles on sports medicine and training. Available at most UK railway-station bookstalls.

Runners' World, Box 366, Mountain View, California 94042 (UK: PO Box 247, Croydon, Surrey, CR9 8AQ)
A leading US publication dealing mainly with the US scene. Available in the UK on subscription.

Running Magazine, 5—8 Lower John Street, London W12 4HA
Published monthly. News, views and race advertisements included. Very interesting articles and training tips. Occasional training weekends are organised. Also a comprehensive advertising section for running-kit shops and mail-order suppliers.

Running Review, 2 Tower Street, Hyde, Cheshire
Published monthly. Race reports, news, views and observations from the UK and elsewhere, plus regular articles on diet, training and injury prevention and therapy. Available on subscription or from selected sports shops.

BOOKS

Barrett, T., and Morissey, R., Jr.: *Marathon Runners*, Messner, New York, 1981
Bloom, M.: *The Marathon: What It Takes to Run the Distance*, Holt, Rinehart and Winston, New York, 1981
Brasher, C.: *The Marathon*, Hodder and Stoughton, London, 1981
Brown, S., and Graham, J.: *Target 26*, Collier-Macmillan, London, 1979
Campbell, G.: *Marathon: The World of the Long-Distance Athlete*, Oak Tree Publications, New York, 1977
Henderson, J. (ed.): *The Complete Marathoner* (3rd edn.), California Mountain View, Anderson World Inc., California, 1981
Hill, R.: *The Long Hard Road* (Parts 1 & 2), Ron Hill Sports Ltd., 1981/1982
Hopkins, J.: *The Marathon*, Stanley Paul, London, 1966
Martin, D. E., and Gynn, R. W.: *The Marathon Foot-Race: Performers and Performances*, Charles C. Thomas, Springfield, Illinois, 1979
Milvy, P. (ed.): *The Long-Distance Athlete: A Definitive Study*, Urizen Press, New York, 1978
Neutl, J. (ed. H. Schroeder): *Marathon Running*, Crestwood House, Minnesota, 1980
Rodgers, W., and Concannon, J.: *Marathoning*, Simon and Schuster, New York, 1980
Steffny, M.: *Marathoning* (3rd edn.), California Mountain View, Anderson World Inc., California, 1981
Sullivan, G.: *Marathon: The Longest Race*, Westminster Press, Philadelphia, Pennsylvania, 1981
Temple, C.: *Challenge of the Marathon*, Stanley Paul, London, 1982
Wilson, N., Etchells, A., and Tulloh, B.: *The Marathon Book*, Virgin Books, London, 1982

Acknowledgements

The authors wish to thank:

Bill Domoney, Sheffield, a 2:19 marathon runner formerly coached by one of the authors, for looking at Chapter 2 from a runner's viewpoint;

Dr Mike H. Harrison, of the RAF Institute of Aviation Medicine, Farnborough, Hampshire, for reading and commenting on Chapter 3;

Dr Anne E. de Looy, of the Department of Health and Applied Sciences, Leeds Polytechnic, for providing Tables 1, 2 and 3 in Chapter 4;

and — last but by no means least — Thelma Holman, for typing the majority of the manuscript.

The authors and publishers wish to acknowledge with thanks the following for permission to reproduce copyright material.

DIAGRAMS

Fig 1. R. Margaria: 'The sources of muscular energy', *Scientific American*, March, 1972

Fig 2. E. J. Burke and J. H. L. Humphreys: *Fit to Exercise*, Pelham Books, 1982

Figs 3, 4, 12. E. L. Fox: *Sports Physiology*, W. B. Saunders, 1972

Fig 5. D. L. Costill: 'Physiology of marathon running', *JAMA*, August, 1972

Fig 6. T. Strasser: 'Coronary risk factors revisited', *World Health Forum*, 1982

Fig 7. Dr J. H. Wilmore, University of Arizona, Tucson, Arizona

Fig 8. E. J. Burke (ed.): *Toward an Understanding of Human Performance* (2nd edn.), Mouvement Publications, 1980

Figs 9, 11. R. J. Shepherd, *The Fit Athlete*, Oxford University Press, 1978

Fig 10. D. L. Costill: 'A scientific approach to distance running', *Track and Field News*, 1979

Fig 13. R. J. Shepherd: *Endurance Fitness*

Fig 15. William McArdle and Frank I. Katch: *Energy, Nutrition and Human Performance*, Lea and Febiger, 1981

Fig 16. J. Bergström: Diet, Muscle Glycogen and Physical Performance, *Acta Physiol. Scand.*, Vol. 71, 140, 1967

Fig 17. E. L. Fox: *Sports Physiology*, W. B. Saunders, 1972; based on data from Karlsson and Saltin (1971)

Fig 18. *Ciba Clinical Symposia*, Vol. 32 No. 4, Ciba Pharmaceuticals, 1980

TABLES

Table 1 Adapted from American College of Sports Medicine: *Guidelines for Graded Exercise Testing and Exercise Prescription* (2nd edn.), Lea & Febiger, Philadelphia, 1980. Reproduced by permission of the publisher

Table 2 Reproduced by permission of the American Heart Association from *Exercise Testing and Training of Individuals with Heart Disease or at High Risk for its Development: A Handbook for Physicians*, Table 5, page 44. Copyright © 1975 by the Committee on Exercise, American Heart Association

Table 3 Reproduced by permission of the American College of Sports Medicine

Table 5 Copyright © 1983 by the Metropolitan Life Insurance Company Reproduced by permission.

Table 6 From *The Aerobics Way* by Kenneth H. Cooper, copyright © 1977. Reprinted by permission of the publishers, M. Evans & Co., New York

Table 13 Adapted from an article in *New Runner's Diet* (World Publications, 1977): 'Fluids for athletic performance: why and what you should drink during prolonged exercise' by D. L. Costill

Table 18 Adapted from N. J. Smith: *Food for Sport*, Bull Publishing Co., Palo Alto, California, 1976. Reproduced by permission of the publisher

Table 19 From N. J. Smith: *Food for Sport*, Bull Publishing Co., Palo Alto, California, 1976. Reproduced by permission of the publisher

PHOTOGRAPHS

Nick Brawn 20, 22, 88 (top and middle), 140
Ron Hill Sports Ltd 8, 105
Mark Shearman 2, 12–18, 21, 23, 26, 32–42, 84–87, 88 (bottom), 99, 131–137, 141, 148
Gordon Wilcock 30, 51–78

Index of names and events

157

General index